Tough Calls

Tough Calls

How to Move Beyond Indecision and Good Intentions

Linda D. Henman

BEP BUSINESS EXPERT PRESS

Tough Calls: How to Move Beyond Indecision and Good Intentions

Copyright © Business Expert Press, LLC, 2017.

All rights reserved. No part of this publication may be reproduced, stored in a retrieval system, or transmitted in any form or by any means—electronic, mechanical, photocopy, recording, or any other except for brief quotations, not to exceed 400 words, without the prior permission of the publisher.

First published in 2017 by
Business Expert Press, LLC
222 East 46th Street, New York, NY 10017
www.businessexpertpress.com

ISBN-13: 978-1-63157-690-4 (paperback)
ISBN-13: 978-1-63157-691-1 (e-book)

Business Expert Press Human Resource Management and Organizational Behavior Collection

Collection ISSN: 1946-5637 (print)
Collection ISSN: 1946-5645 (electronic)

Cover and interior design by Exeter Premedia Services Private Ltd., Chennai, India

First edition: 2017

10 9 8 7 6 5 4 3 2 1

Printed in the United States of America.

*To Michele, Patrick, Julie, Andrew, and Matthew,
the best grandkids on the planet.*

Abstract

As my clients began to emerge from the global economic turmoil that began in 2008, they indicated they had learned numerous lessons—the most important one: When leaders make good decisions, little else matters. When they refuse to make decisions, or show a pattern of making bad ones, nothing else matters. As I helped these leaders position themselves for the new economy, I began to see what others didn't see. Something was standing in their way—usually the unwillingness or inability to make a critical decision. In many cases, they thought they needed more—more education, more experience, more time, or more data. They didn't realize they had enough of these, but they did lack the confidence, courage, and optimism to make the tough call.

Through our work together, the most successful leaders realized they could no longer push growth. Instead, they had to remove barriers to success, and usually these barriers were of their own making. They needed to understand how to leverage their strengths and remove their blind spots to move beyond what they thought possible.

These compelling stories and surprising research findings in this book focus on real people who actively sought professional improvement and personal development. Working together, we mapped out their journeys, identified the key roadblocks they faced, recognized the wrong turns they had taken, and unlocked their decision-making potential—all the while navigating an increasingly uncertain world, and in some cases, more than doubling the size of their companies.

Readers will discover that there's much more to decision-making than they ever imagined. They will come away with tools to help them deepen their understanding of what it takes to make tough calls and an understanding of how to inspire others to do the same. Most of these stories illustrate how and why these leaders succeed, but others serve as warnings about what can happen when leaders refuse to decide.

Keywords

decision-making, problem-solving, culture, strategy, espoused beliefs, operating beliefs, self-esteem, optimism, high potentials, humor, trust, persuasion, brainwashing, influence, ethics, organizational judgment, change, motivation

Contents

Introduction xi

Chapter 1 The Le Brea Tar Pit of Good Intentions 1

Part I **Beliefs** **21**

Chapter 2 Sacred Cows Make the Best Burgers 23

Chapter 3 Become the Company That Could Put You Out of Business 45

Chapter 4 A Funny Thing Happened on the Way to the Bottom Line 65

Chapter 5 Brainwashing or Persuasion? 85

Part II **Action** **105**

Chapter 6 Getting More without Settling for Less 107

Chapter 7 Everybody with a Coin to Toss Is Not a Leader ...123

Part III **Results** **141**

Chapter 8 Change Yesterday's Dangerous Ideas 143

Chapter 9 What Motivates Us to Make Tough Calls? 161

Appendix: Your Tough Call Quotient—Your TCQ 177
About the Author 181
Notes 183
References 185
Index 187

Introduction

Walt Disney ignited a fire in the entertainment world that continues to burn brightly decades after his death. Perhaps no single figure has so dominated American, and indeed even global, popular culture the way Walt Disney has and still does. Each year, millions view Disney movies, visit theme parks that bear his name, watch Disney-branded television shows, listen to Disney recordings, buy Disney products, and read books by and about him. He still holds sway in much that has touched our lives, inspiring millions of people and generating billions of dollars.

We cannot measure Disney's influence as a film producer, director, screenwriter, voice actor, animator, entrepreneur, and philanthropist only by numbers or encomia. However, we can state that, most notably, he changed the shape of American recreation with his Disney parks, reconceptualizing the amusement park as an all-encompassing imaginative experience—a *theme park*—rather than a series of diversions, shows, or rides. He made TOUGH CALLS to open Disneyland and then made a series of *additional* TOUGH CALLS to create a chain reaction—a domino effect. We remember Disney as a leader whose influence went beyond his initial area of concentration. He encouraged space exploration, urban planning, and an appreciation of history, context, and perspective. In short, he demonstrated how *one* person can assert his will on the world and "wish upon a star"—to become the leader of the Club he made for you and me.

What could this entertainment icon, a food giant, portfolio managers, and prisoners of war possibly have in common? Each fostered success, not in dramatic responses to crises, but in the unglamorous, unpopular, day-to-day world of TOUGH CALLS. I have built a thriving business working with leaders in these arenas, observing how successful leaders approach TOUGH CALLS and how the *un*successful ones dodge the TOUGH CALLS, make the wrong decisions, or don't keep their jobs long enough to make another one.

Typically, executive leaders define organizations in vast, sweeping generalizations—everything a priority, so *nothing* a priority. Now we're beginning to understand that only *some* parts of a given organization demand the TOUGH CALLS. Which parts? And why do we continue to count things that *don't* count?

TOUGH CALLS has three parts. Part One debunks many of the sacred myths about decision making and looks at the beliefs that drive behavior and create organizational environments. The three chapters in this section challenge readers to examine the sources of their beliefs—to question what they have always thought and the ways they've always done things.

Part Two ties these beliefs to behaviors, especially a leader's most significant actions—making or dodging TOUGH CALLS. The chapters in this section show how and why core beliefs inform our actions in both positive and negative ways. Readers will discover lesser-known wisdom about the role of good judgment in making pivotal decisions and in preventing disastrous ones. I'll share surprising actions readers can take to boost insight, like looking for *themes and patterns* instead of dwelling on individual events, solutions-focused thinking, and outliers.

Part Three establishes how beliefs and actions influence results and offers practical, actionable, empirically supported approaches, calling to mind the early work of Edgar Schein. Decades ago he taught that a change-oriented leader cannot produce change without measurement, but a measurement-oriented leader cannot produce change without a strategy that integrates the measurement of the change process. It all relates to performance, and it all starts with an ability and a willingness to make the TOUGH CALLS—your *TOUGH CALL Quotient*, "TCQ," an assessment that will help you determine how well you make essential decisions.

Although I've based this book on my work with CEOs and their leadership teams, and they remain my primary audience, the theories apply to *everyone* who wants to face life's TOUGH CALLS with more clarity and confidence. Whether you lead a small department within a larger company or simply want to improve your approach to making decisions, you can enjoy more success when you start making TOUGH CALLS better.

Even though we remember him as an entertainment genius, Disney offers a modern-day gold standard for organizational development. He taught us that strong leaders don't shy away from the TOUGH CALLS, fearing that they will make the wrong ones or that others will second-guess them. He realized a quest for perfection or the approval of others stands at cross-purposes with success.

Walt Disney and others of his ilk ... Steve Jobs, Jack Welch, Lee Iacocca ... committed the sin of making TOUGH CALLS without worrying about what others thought—the same TOUGH CALLS that positioned these men and their companies for greatness. They remind us that ineffective leadership seldom results from rusty management skills. Similarly, organizational disasters and triumphs usually don't occur because of a flawed culture. Both happen when imperfect leaders fail to make the TOUGH CALLS—when they ignore the links among beliefs, actions, and results.

Philosopher John Dewey observed, "Saints engage in introspection while burly sinners run the world." The author offers this book to burly sinners—those leaders who make the TOUGH CALLS because they realize failure is instructive and smart people learn as much from failures as they do from successes.

CHAPTER 1

The Le Brea Tar Pit of Good Intentions

For tens of thousands of years, oil seepage from the earth created craters of pitch in urban Los Angeles, known as the Le Brea Tar Pits. The tar formed a deposit thick enough to trap unsuspecting animals that wandered in, became trapped, and eventually died. Predators ventured in to eat the ensnared animals and found themselves stuck, too. Over many centuries, the Le Brea Tar Pits have trapped and preserved the remains of animals that once roamed the earth with pride and distinction—the victims of Mother Nature, other marauders, and their own bad judgment.

Many of the remains in the tar pits are those of giant sloths—elephant-sized mammals that moved so slowly they provided the habitat to other organisms. A single sloth, for example, provided a home for moths, beetles, cockroaches, fungi, and algae. Sloths move only when necessary and then very slowly. They spend the bulk of their time eating from a single tree, from which they move only to breed or to find another tree. Sometimes they don't even bother to breed, so some species have now become extinct. The metaphors for 21st century organizations invite comparison.

Ineffective leadership seldom happens because of rusty management skills. Similarly, organizational disasters usually don't occur because of a flawed culture. No, poor leadership and corporate disasters happen when leaders persist in sloth-like approaches, ignoring the links among beliefs, decision making, and results. Leaders need a new approach for thinking about the environment of the organization—a new ideology that inexorably links decision making, organizational environment, and success.

Doing Violence to Good Sense

How many organic growth initiatives and failed acquisitions have happened since the 2008 downturn? Today we see a landscape littered with thousands of corporate carcasses. Like their unsuspecting prehistoric animal counterparts who sought only food and water in the deceptively attractive tar pits, these organizations wandered aimlessly into the quicksand of bad decisions—victimizing themselves and making themselves prey to fickle customers, competitor takeovers, and attrition of talent—all the while blaming "culture" both inside and outside the organization for their troubles. The slow-moving sloths among them that refused to make essential decisions suffered disproportionately because they either couldn't or wouldn't make the tough calls that would have saved them.

Yet, people continue to bat around the word "culture" as though it were a conversational shuttlecock. When an individual, merger, or organization fails, culture takes the blame. We use the word somewhat arbitrarily, citing it to explain why things don't change, won't change, or can't change. "Culture" becomes that subtle-yet-powerful driver that leaders strive—often futilely—to influence.

Creating an organizational powerhouse requires more—more analysis, more in-depth understanding of self-initiated traps, and more awareness of the role external snares can play in jeopardizing success. It all starts with tough calls that address dilemmas.

Traditionally, business leaders defined corporate culture as the pattern of shared assumptions that a group adopted and adapted over a period of time to solve problems and adjust to the world around them. When something worked well, and leaders considered it valid, members of the organization began to teach the behavior to new people. Through this process, new members found out what those around them thought and felt about issues that touched the organization. These perceptions helped coordinate activity tacitly—without communicating too much or thinking too much. "Culture" offered a simple defense for just about everything but explained almost nothing important—like business results.

Those of us in the trenches developed codes, jargon, symbols, rules, and norms to share our assumptions about what would and should happen, and we raised each new litter of newcomers to embrace both the artifacts and the assumptions—all the while ignoring success. Largely HR-driven, explaining culture started as a well-intended attempt to understand how humans work together but gradually morphed into a modern-day La Brea Tar Pit where good intentions go to die amid all the dinosaurs and fossilized specimens of organizational decisions.

Blaming recent failed mergers and acquisitions on incompatible cultures sped up the setting of the trap. Leaders blamed "culture," but faulty decision making and good old-fashioned bad judgment played roles, too. Soon, *patterns* of bad judgment—those things that don't work but that people resist changing because "we've always done it that way"—materialized. The culture trap took the form of antilearning, antichange, and eventually, antisuccess. The trap created blinders we continue to call "culture."

A paradox emerged. On one hand, most agree this trap compromised effective performance. On the other hand, we focused very little on what leaders could do to prevent or manage past the trap in the first place. We need new ways of thinking about the environment of the organization—new ways to describe and understand organizational traps—new ways that will help us design and implement interventions that reduce or eliminate them.

In his classic novel *Anna Karenina*, Tolstoy stated that every happy family is alike; every unhappy family is unhappy in its own way. Tolstoy meant that, in order to be considered happy, a family must succeed in critical respects: attraction between the husband and wife, agreement on key decisions related to child-rearing, money, and other vital issues. Failure in any one of these essential respects can doom a family, even if its members have all the other ingredients needed for happiness. Unfortunately, family members cannot solve their problems one at a time. On the contrary, all the problems interconnect, and family members must address them concurrently. Failure to do so provokes unhappiness. Unbeknownst to him, Tolstoy created the first family systems theory and an organizational development theory, too.

From this came "The Anna Karenina Principle," a belief that posits: In order for an organizational endeavor to succeed, the people involved must avoid every possible deficiency. The principle, therefore, implies that success is more elusive than failure. Success reflects a perfect storm of contributors. The absence of only *one* of these significant contributors precludes the positive, desirable, or worthy.

Conversely, we have a banquet of options for harming an organization: greed, inadequate leadership, poor performance, faulty decision making, external pressures, and so on, making the road to failure wide and varied. Yet, too often, business leaders seek easy, single-factor explanations for success—and too often they conclude "culture" provides that single-factor explanation. To meet most important goals, however, success actually requires avoiding many separate possible causes of failure.

Jared Diamond popularized the Anna Karenina Principle in his bestseller, *Guns, Germs and Steel*. The author used the principle to illustrate why so few wild animals have been successfully domesticated throughout history. A deficiency in any one of a great number of factors can render a species undomesticable, he said. Therefore, we don't consider all successfully domesticated species domesticated because of a particular *positive* trait, but because of a lack of any number of negative traits such as limited diet, slow growth rate, nasty dispositions, loner tendencies, and so on.[1]

In nature and in business, myriad and unlimited reasons exist for failure—opportunities for success remain more limited. Missing a target is easy, hitting it more difficult. None of this implies that leaders should pursue perfection. On the contrary, perfection will continue to serve as the archenemy of both success and excellence. Successful change does require a mindset shift—a new way of looking at the organization's environment—a realization that success has more to do with how a company makes money than how it clings to its "culture."

Think of culture as organizational health and happiness. You can infer health from robust activity and demeanor. You can perceive a damaged culture from what people say, what they do, and what others say about them. We can embrace the few markers of organizational health while we simultaneously combat the many threats to this health. Political correctness would have us believe no culture qualifies as right or wrong, better or worse, except in relation to what the organization aspires to accomplish.

The facts tell a different story. Gone are the days of *describing* what happens in organizations, here to stay times of *prescribing* what must happen for success. A new recipe for results has emerged, but not everyone has lost a taste for the old one.

Legends tend to have differing adaptations; the truth has no versions. Both influence—either intentionally or unintentionally—the organizations we build. Corporate culture—the pattern of shared assumptions that the group has adopted and adapted over a period of time—develops in much the same way legends and traditions do. Edgar Schein, the father of cultural awareness, defined culture as the visible structures and process he called artifacts, espoused values, and unconscious assumptions.[2]

Artifacts include all the phenomena we see, hear, and feel when we encounter a group or enter the front doors of an organization. They include the visible products of the groups, such as the physical environment, language, technology, products, clothing, manner of address, stories, and observed ritual.

In most organizations, leaders give considerable thought to espoused values. These values may appear on a plaque in the foyer or on a mouse pad, but successful leaders also model them. Values play an important role in forming an organization's culture because senior leaders agree, "This is the way we do things around here."

Unconscious assumptions remain more mysterious, lying below the surface, undetected but ready to influence outcomes both positively and negatively. In damaged organizations, unconscious assumptions commonly contradict the espoused values, causing confusion within and without the company. They also engender mistrust, suspicion, and, eventually, the loss of customers and star performers. Schein's definition sheds preliminary light on what helps and hinders organizational success, but it doesn't go far enough because artifacts, values, and assumptions don't occur in a vacuum. They interact continuously and profoundly over time to influence behaviors that eventually determine outcomes, creating the need for a new way of defining organizational systems and avoiding the tar pit of good intentions.

The Anatomy of Tough Calls

When a solution to a problem works repeatedly, people start to take it for granted. The hypothesis, supported originally only by a hunch, gradually comes to be treated as a certainty. Basic assumptions become so ingrained no one challenges them. For example, years ago senior HR leaders may have implemented a process the company should use for firing—a policy they assured leaders would "keep us out of trouble." Through the years, the policy morphed into a ridiculous pattern of paying unproductive employees severance pay to keep them from suing the company. Now, years later, the company makes a practice of paying the unproductive people they need to fire instead of using those funds to attract top talent to replace them. People assume the company must continue to pay people they fire. Eventually these kinds of beliefs become embedded in an ideology or organizational philosophy that serves as a guide for dealing with ambiguity, difficult events, or sudden changes.

When leaders continually and constantly grapple with the tough questions and develop a list of standards that serves as more than a pretty poster on the wall, these beliefs serve as the bedrock of the organization's strategy and provide guidelines about how and what to change and what everyone needs to learn in the process. When beliefs veer from espoused values and create a dysfunctional set of standards, the opposite occurs; and people start behaving in ways that hurt the organization.

However, when leaders understand the importance of making tough, often unpopular calls, and then have the courage to do so, organizational excellence can take root. Successful tough calls have four constructs: moral gyroscope, sound judgment, fortitude, and experience.

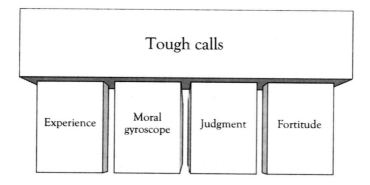

A gyroscope is an apparatus that consists of a rotating wheel mounted on an axis so that it can spin freely in all directions. Tilting of the mounting and movements of surrounding parts do not affect the orientation of the axis, so it can provide stability, provide equilibrium, and maintain an absolute reference direction in navigation systems, automatic pilots, and stabilizers.

Like its navigational counterpart, a strong moral gyroscope provides the same sort of stability and direction in the midst of chaos and moving parts. However, a *moral* gyroscope demands that leaders *do* something, not that they merely *be* in a state or condition of integrity. Making tough calls successfully involves those lifelong activities that *actualize* ethics and integrity. In business, the difficult and controversial question arises when we ask whether certain benefits qualify as more desirable than others. This effective engagement of a moral gyroscope involves a search for the *highest* good, which has three characteristics:

We deem the action desirable.
We deem it desirable itself, not for the sake of some *other* good.
All other benefits are desirable for the sake of the action.

Deontology, from the Greek *deon*, which means "obligation" or "duty," judges the morality of an action based on the action's adherence to rules—required, forbidden, or permitted choices. This school of thought posits that some acts are *inherently* ethical or unethical, irrespective of legality, pragmatics, or common practice. Philosophers commonly contrast deontological ethics with consequentialist ethics—that is, the rightness of an action is determined by its consequences. Many excuse behaviors that would ordinarily seem wrong but which they collectively forgive when done for the betterment of the organization. This wrongminded approach makes tough calls even tougher.

Integrity is a not a raincoat you put on when the business climate indicates you should. Integrity creates a condition that guides your life—not just a set of protocols. Courageous leaders don't acquire their moral gyroscopes solely by learning general rules. They also develop them—those deliberative, emotional, and social skills that enable them to put their understanding of integrity into practice in suitable ways—through practice. Similarly, these leaders understand that they can't "teach" ethics to others by requiring their signatures on a statement. Instead, they *exemplify* and model ethics in their personal and professional lives, and experience teaches them how to reapply their ethics to tough calls as those tough calls emerge.

Experience gives us a respect for history without making us starstruck by it, shackled to it, or straightjacketed by it. Experience allows us to put previous decisions in perspective, to realize that never failing also means never taking appropriate risks or playing in a tough enough league. Experience also teaches us that tough calls come more often by imposition than invitation. Captain Sullenberger probably felt that way when he successfully landed U.S. Airways Flight 1549 in the Hudson River on January 15, 2009, saving the lives of 155 people. He didn't "invite" that tough call. Circumstances "imposed" it.

In 2009 Sullenberger, a senior captain, boasted more than 19,000 hours of flying time he had accumulated in his more than 30 years of flying experience. In interviews and writings after the crash, Sullenberger credited his vast experience in both flying and safety for his ability to do what he had to do on that January day. Could he have done it with fewer hours of flying time? We'll never know. The question, therefore, remains, "How much experience do we need to make the tough calls?" Perhaps the depth of the person's fortitude offers the answer.

Psychological research tells us that people who overcome adversity build confidence and self-esteem that tells them they can do it again. When we repeatedly play the cards we're dealt, overcome obstacles, and emerge unscathed, or at least still in one piece, the experience tells us we can do it again.

The Marines have known this since their inception. That's why they build adversity into their boot camps and training programs. They intentionally *manufacture* adversity. They produce and control the adversity and teach recruits the skills to prevail over and through it. After they face and clear the obstacles a number of times over the span of several months, the would-be marines have the experience to realize they can face and defend against the same kinds of dangers and difficulties in similar, if not the same situations. The combination of experience and fortitude equips them to make tough calls at a certain level, but then the role of judgment comes into play.

A marine sergeant doesn't have the luxury of calling a meeting to discuss options and build consensus as the enemy comes over the hill. He must act decisively and bravely to apply his training to a situation he has not encountered in exactly the same way as the one he faces. His life and the lives of those in his chain of command quite literally depend on his ability to make a tough call—and get it right . . . right now.

In my more than 35 years of consulting in the business arena, I have found, without question, sound judgment ranks as the single most significant differentiator between those who can make successful tough calls and those who cannot. While fortitude addresses a *willingness* to make tough calls, judgment involves the *ability* to make them. Specifically, the most crucial forecaster of executive success involves advanced critical thinking skills—the specific cognitive abilities that equip us to solve problems, make effective decisions, and keep a global perspective. These abilities equip a leader to anticipate future consequences, to get to the core of complicated issues, and to zero in on the essential few while putting aside the trivial many.

Biographers tell us Steve Jobs didn't always demonstrate great people skills, but his track record indicates he had highly developed analytical reasoning skills that enabled him to make tough calls. He simply demanded that his team come up with "the next best thing." Jobs could trace both his success and failure to the same root element: his refusal to accept that the bounds of reality applied to him. He and his team did the impossible because Jobs didn't perceive any limits to what he and his team could learn and do.

After Jobs's return to Apple in 1997, he oversaw the development of the iMac, iTunes, iPod, iPhone, and iPad, and directed the establishment of Apple Retail Stores, iTunes Store, and the App Store. The success of these products and services—a series of tough calls—provided several years of stable financial returns and propelled Apple to become the world's most valuable publicly-traded company in 2011. Many regard the reinvigoration of the company one of the greatest turnarounds in business history. We will remember Steve Jobs for his enormous successes, but what about the "Lisa"? Setbacks didn't stop Jobs.

Leaders like Steve Jobs learn from their mistakes—all the while encouraging others to go through the inevitable cycle of the pain of failing, learning, and changing. As the world becomes more complex and interdependent, sound judgment—the ability to think systematically and to understand cause/effect relationships, becomes more critical to both learning and change.

When companies embrace a change orientation, they consider the tough calls that lead to innovation part of the way they do business, not a process or project they engage in for a given period of time. People innovate when they see a benefit—when they perceive that the change will improve their condition, not when someone *else* wants it. The following questions will help determine your results orientation:

- Do we make decisions we can implement immediately?
  Or, do we "vet" decisions to every conceivable stakeholder, suggesting we seek their "buy in," when we actually want their approval? Every year one of my clients loses a sterling opportunity because of delayed decision making—artificially created setbacks that cost mightily. Most recently, a president missed an opportunity to hire an industry star because he wanted others to meet the candidate. Travel schedules interfered with progress; speed did not seem of the essence. While the client wasted precious time, a competitor made an offer, and the candidate accepted. Now this star shines in another galaxy—that of the competition.
- To what extent will employees accept leader-only or expert-only decisions?
  While often desirable, consensus simply takes too long, and it ignores or negates a leader's often more trustworthy intuition. Successful organizations realize they have to outrun the competition, but they have to do more. They must also exceed their customers' expectations. These kinds of tough calls require both speed and agility. An aircraft carrier will never be able to turn with the nimbleness of a speedboat; therefore, visionary leaders delegate important decisions to the most qualified person on the team, or they make them themselves. I've never been a fan of consensus, and each passing year and missed opportunity confirms my distaste for it. Today's changing economy simply won't allow companies to take the time to involve everyone in everything.

- How adeptly do we evaluate risk?
  Smart risk-takers define the playing field for everyone else. We won't soon forget the greatness of Steve Jobs. He anticipated and imagined the next big thing and then provided it. He didn't ask consumers what we wanted; he just invented what he knew we *needed*. Do you have the thinkers within your organization who can take your company to the edge of the cliff without letting it tumble over? Or, do your risk managers assume the role of business-prevention managers?
- How comfortable would we feel about giving up the status quo?
  What parts would we miss? What can't we live without? So-called comfort food makes us fat, and parts of the status quo make us lazy. We become ego-involved in the way we've always done things—imagining our entire world will fall off its axis if we admit to learning and leading a better way.
- How have and how will market changes demand that we change?
  Sometimes external factors make a decision for us. September 11 changed forever the way we travel, and no one expected or anticipated these changes. Yet, our economy demanded that we figure it out and get planes and passengers back in the air. Again, sometimes change comes more from imposition than invitation, but an agile culture can position an organization to respond well either way.
- How well does the speed we prefer match the pace the market demands?
  To remain competitive and exceptional, a culture must foster and embrace incentives, agility, rewards, experimentation, and high-risk tolerance, not quick victories. Many organizations demanding more "innovation" simply want faster problem-solving, which will only return things to the status quo but not actually force leaders to make the tough calls that would change anything important.

To distinguish between decision making and problem-solving, think of solving problems as the process of finding a solution to something that needs to change or a deviation from what you expected to happen. It requires a multistage process for moving an issue or situation from an undesirable state to a more advantageous condition and typically involves a process for answering the following questions:

What changed? When? What caused the change?
What tangible evidence do we have that we have a problem?
How can we measure the magnitude of the problem?
Does it matter? In other words, do we consider this change or deviation consequential enough to spend time resolving it?

Once you have the answers to these questions, you can start evaluating alternatives and overcoming the obstacles that stand between them and a satisfactory resolution. Leaders have many ways to do this, but too many organizations engage in ongoing problem-solving, usually returning things to the status quo and seldom making the tough calls—seldom embracing real innovation and change.

For example, in an attempt to understand why one of his divisions had lost productivity and morale, the head of a large hospital purchased four different surveys. Each said the same thing: "There's a big problem here." The VP searched tirelessly for a cure—anything that would return things to the division's previous condition and help him avoid the tough decisions he needed to make. We discussed several of his alternatives: implement a new performance review process, give feedback to the employees who had stopped attending "mandatory" meetings, and change the requirements for answering emails.

After his attempts to solve all the problems, I said, "Jim, you're just rearranging the deck chairs on the Titanic. All the data point to one conclusion: Rob (division leader) isn't a strong leader and either can't or won't ever be. He needs to retire, and you need to find his replacement." In this case, innovation came with the change and a tough call. Leaders like Jim should measure their organizational climate in one way and only one way—results. What outputs do you want and expect? Are you getting them? The answers to these questions will position you to storm the castle of your competitors.

Evidence That You Haven't Faced the Dilemma

Playing the role of Monday-morning-quarterback requires no real skill or experience. A superficial knowledge of football seems to help, but many an "expert" has sat in an armchair and told others what *should a* happened, never able to articulate what occurred to cause the problems. Those who have responsibility for understanding business decisions don't do much better. They can most assuredly assign blame, and many can adeptly conduct an accident investigation, but too few see or heed the early warning signs.

In *Landing in the Executive Chair,* I encouraged readers to heed the early warning signs that they may be heading for a crisis. I have reframed some of the points I offered in that book to pinpoint the 10 indicators that warn leaders they're failing to make the tough calls. That failure can lead to loss of productivity in the short run and crisis in the long run.

Ten Signs You Need to Make Some Tough Calls

1. An inability among senior leaders to articulate the organization's strategy

   Most leaders can tell you what they plan to do this week or this quarter, but fewer have the ability to put into words exactly why the company does what it does, how they make money, where they want to be in five years, and what differentiates them from the competition. Too often this inability to communicate the vision, mission, and strategy comes from a reluctance or inability to make tough calls accurately and quickly. Winning coaches can't dawdle in the middle of a big game. They know the clock ticks away their opportunities as quickly as they surface.

2. No clarity about or accountability for decisions (and/or no apparent penalties for indecision)

   Often organizational dithering happens when leaders don't understand exactly what decisions they should make. Too often, I see clients miss an opportunity when they took too long making the call. Both candidates for hire and opportunities disappear when all major decisions require consensus, or when leaders fear the consequences of their calls. Indecision usually carries no immediate penalty, so it becomes the default position, with finger-pointing and blame acting as the backup systems.

3. Inappropriate risk-taking

I have often said a leader's second-worst nightmare is an idiot with initiative—their first being a smart sociopath. Either group tends to take excessive risks, sometimes because they don't know better; often because they enjoy the rush of the uncertainty. Leaders don't want to incur fines or other adverse regulatory events, and neither do they benefit when they tolerate code of conduct violations.

A paradox emerges. On one hand, no company can fund recklessness for very long. On the other hand, most breakthroughs come from risk-taking and innovation, so risk aversion can cripple a company nearly as much as excessive risk-taking can. Successful leaders learn quickly that they must make the tough calls that balance innovation and caution, and they need to leave the risky tough calls to the smartest, best-informed people in the room.

4. Financial problems

Financial problems can take many obvious forms: lower margins, reduced market share, no return on investment, etc. Usually an obvious, or at least a clear answer, will solve these kinds of problems, but the truly tough financial calls involve less measurable quantifiers.

For instance, one client made the financial decision to pursue 2 percent margin work in one market when other markets tended to yield 5 percent margins. The reason? The lower-margin work addressed other priorities, like providing cash flow. The higher-margin work wouldn't last if employees couldn't count on a paycheck every month, so the CEO made the tough call to balance both priorities. This kind of willingness to deviate from established practices helps explain how and why this particular construction company thrived during the economic downturn.

5. "Workarounds" or other deviations from protocols

Every year—and by that I mean every single year—since I've been in the consulting business, I have encountered an impressive "workaround," a deviation from best practices and standard protocols.

Sometimes the workaround takes the form of a senior person cleaning up after someone in a subordinate position. This year, I have encountered more "pass the trash" among clients—a specific workaround term that clients use that describes moving rather than firing an unproductive employee.

One large hospital has engaged in so much of it this past year that getting fired has become nearly impossible. Their HR department has established THE most incredibly complex and idiotic system for firing that I've ever encountered. An "at-risk" employee has six—that's right—six chances to improve in a year. Even if the problematic behavior (absenteeism, low productivity, etc.) doesn't improve with the first five warnings, the employee still has one remaining shot at staying employed. Does anyone have to guess about the financial condition of this organization? This hospital has moved beyond a quandary to create a quagmire.

6. Persistent complaints

    Consider the first complaint—whether from customers, vendors, or employees—an outlier. Think of the second as a coincidence and the third as a pattern. Once you see the pattern, it's time for a tough call. Failure to make the call after the third complaint will likely lead to the loss of key customers and/or star performers.

7. A preponderance of rumors

    Just as they should be cautious about complaints, leaders should listen to rumors with more than a grain of salt. Look for objective evidence before dignifying any rumor with a reaction. But when you encounter a preponderance of rumors, and evidence begins to surface of their veracity, time to act.

8. Lack of innovation or reluctance to change

    Most people love the status quo because they think it doesn't hurt. While not perfect, doing what we've always done in the same way that we've always done it requires so much less angst and energy than experimenting with new approaches or pressing for innovative ideas.

    Tolerating and rewarding rigidity eventually creates its own punishment—but often not before it encourages an inability to learn from mistakes. Creating an environment of learning requires a series of tough calls designed to reward effort, not just success.

9. Turnover among star performers or no one ready for promotion

   Stars force people to take them seriously. They don't raise the bar—they set it for everyone else. They serve as gold standards of what people should strive to be and what they should attain. You wouldn't hesitate to hire them again, and you'd be crushed if you found out they had accepted another position. They give generously but expect repayment in kind.

   When a star leaves, take note. The departure probably means someone in a position of authority made the wrong call or failed to make a tough call. Stars will explain your success as an organization, but they will demand excellence in return: excellent management, financial stability, a clear strategy, a fair fleshed-out succession plan, and top-notch fellow employees with whom they will work.

10. Damaged brand

    Damage to a brand usually happens subtly and silently over a period of time—a sudden loss of repute in the industry among customers or among future talent, more rarely. So, leaders often fail to realize the damage until it's too late. Addressing the aforementioned nine categories of tough calls can help prevent the tough luck that usually follows an inability or unwillingness to *make* the tough calls.

The Predicament That Follows

When leaders make the wrong calls or fail to make the tough calls on important issues, after a period of time, consequences start to emerge. To protect their patterns of behavior, leaders start to censor their own thoughts and convince themselves they aren't doing so. The next logical step in this downward spiral involves making their decisions off limits to scrutiny. In what I call "Defense of the Sacred," leaders make even the mere mention or criticism of one of their decisions a sacrilege. That's what happened with the priest scandals in the Catholic Church.

Although allegations of priest abuse trace their origins back decades, if not centuries, the first accusations began to surface publicly in the United States in the late 1980s. Cases against the church's hierarchy who hadn't reported the abuse to legal authorities came to light about the same time—survivors claiming church leaders had deliberately moved sexually abusive priests to other parishes where the abuse often continued. These initial cover-ups did three things: they perpetuated the abuse; they built mistrust in the system; and they invited fraud cases when it came to light that the Catholic Church had deliberately relocated priests when victims believed the priests had been removed from placements with children.

The cases subsequently received overwhelming media attention throughout the world, prompting church officials to argue that the coverage was both excessive and disproportionate. The allegations, the media coverage, and the lawsuits that followed combined to create a perfect PR nightmare. Eventually reports of the billions of dollars in settlements to victims joined the fray in what a Vatican official in 2011 called a "ludicrous publicity stunt and a misuse of international judicial processes."[3]

Since the Vatican official made this proclamation, dioceses have declared bankruptcy, parishes have perished; schools have closed; and several bishops and one pope have resigned. This "ludicrous publicity stunt" has had far-reaching and dire consequences that continue to haunt the Catholic Church—and that doesn't begin to account for the ruined lives of the people who suffered the abuse. As a Catholic, I find my church's defense both ludicrous and sad.

Secular organizations defend the sacred more often than religious groups do. In 2011 a jury convicted Penn State's former assistant football coach Jerry Sandusky on 52 counts of child molestation. Once again, the "Defense of the Sacred" mindset resulted in considerable collateral damage. Because officials at Penn State had failed to notify law enforcement after learning of Sandusky's abusive behavior, school president Graham Spanier, athletic director Tim Curley, and longtime head football coach Joe Paterno all lost their jobs and forever sullied their reputations.

Joe Paterno had been the head coach at Penn State from 1966 until 2011 with 409 victories, making him the winningest coach in Football Bowl Subdivision history, but we will remember him for his role in the Sandusky scandal. Why? Because he defended the sacred—in this case, the religiosity associated with defending the sanctity of football at Penn State and his own good name. The story drips with irony.

Deflecting decisions in a misguided attempt to defend the sacred is one way to invite the gnashing of teeth into an organization.

Chauvinistic adherence to one of the top three: quality, money, or speed illustrates another. That explains what happened in the Atlanta public schools.

In 2015, in what many have described as the largest cheating scandal to rock the nation's public education system, authorities indicted 35 Atlanta Public School educators and administrators on charges of racketeering and corruption. Prosecutors alleged that, in an effort to bolster student test scores for financial reward, the defendants conspired to either cheat, conceal cheating, or retaliate against whistleblowers. Prosecutors found evidence that the cheating dated back as far as 2005.

The former superintendent of Atlanta Public Schools, Beverly Hall, was among the educators charged in the scandal. Hall had resigned from her position in 2011 after a state investigation into large, unexplained test score gains in some Atlanta schools. Hall denied any role in the cheating scandal, even though a state review determined cheating had occurred in more than half of the district's elementary and middle schools. Investigators accused Dr. Hall of creating "a culture of fear, intimidation and retaliation that permitted cheating at all levels to go unchecked for years."[4] Hall died in March of 2015 before she could stand trial but not before her name would live in infamy.

Twenty-one of the accused reached plea agreements before the trial, but then the courts convicted 11 of the 12 teachers involved of racketeering, each receiving either a prison sentence, a fine, probation, community service, or a combination of them all—the "severe consequences" the judge had promised.

Whether defending the sacred or chauvinistically adhering to a measure of success, leaders incite tragedy or at least riotous bad luck when they protect their patterns of behavior, stifle their own reservations, repress their beliefs, or otherwise do violence to good sense. They create a modern-day La Brea Tar Pit where both good and bad intentions go to die.

Conclusion

When John Dewey observed "Saints engage in introspection while burly sinners run the world," I know he didn't have the Catholic Church hierarchy, Penn State officials, or the superintendent of the Atlanta Public Schools in mind. While, arguably, all sinners, they also did violence to good sense and failed profoundly and promiscuously to learn from mistakes.

While Dewey's quote may cause a reader to infer that saints err in introspection, I doubt he implied that leaders should avoid deliberation either. They shouldn't. Corporate disasters happen when leaders persist in sloth-like approaches to the tough calls they face. Success starts with contemplation of one's beliefs—it just shouldn't end there. It should progress with alacrity and dispatch to the tough calls that will keep an organization out of both the trenches and the tar pits.

PART I
Beliefs

CHAPTER 2

Sacred Cows Make the Best Burgers

No one seems to agree about the origin of the term "sacred cow." Before it emerged as an idiom in America in the latter part of the 19th century, some believe the term simply described the elevated place cows enjoyed in Hinduism. Or, the term may have originated with the legendary hero, Prithu, who assumed the form of a cow to encourage his subjects to raise more vegetables. But some also accuse Prithu of chasing and capturing the earth goddess Prithvi, who fled in the form of a cow and eventually agreed to yield her milk to feed the world. Greeks and Egyptians also have their own references to goddesses who took the form of cows. As often happens with legends and organizational myths, history gets messy. About this, however, everyone seems to agree: In modern usage, the term "sacred cow" refers to an idea or practice people consider, often unreasonably, immune to question or criticism. The "Defense of the Sacred" examples in chapter 1 explain the consequences of this practice.

We revere our sacred cows for several reasons. Most important, they help us avoid embarrassment, surprises, and threats. Even when employees show great competency in a particular skill, they often show *greater* expertise in protecting what they hold dear. After a while, leaders build corrals for their sacred cows—organizational black holes where everyone repeats the hallowed mantra, "We must win. We must not lose," even if experimenting could eventually lead to much bigger success.

When people in an organization deem a topic off-limits, they eliminate scrutiny, evaluation, and measurement as they stick with what they've always considered sacrosanct. They tie their own hands and limit their opportunities for growth, success, and job fulfillment. But when they *question* "holy teachings" as part of their day-to-day operations, they unleash their potential to solve problems in new ways, approach challenges with optimism, and simultaneously boost their corporate self-esteem and fill their coffers. Killing sacred cows is the first step, cooking them with a new tough-call recipe, the second.

Don't Take Risks; Create Them

BAR (Beliefs, Actions, and Results) offers a new way to think about the environment of the organization—an ecosystem where people embrace risk, and excellence prevails amid fortitude and good judgment. Beliefs reflect those perceptions leaders consider "correct." Over time, the group learns that certain beliefs work to reduce indecision and doubt in critical areas of the organization's functioning. As leaders continue to support these beliefs, and the beliefs continue to work, they gradually transform into an articulated set of more engrained beliefs, norms, and operational rules of behavior.

Corporate beliefs describe the principles and standards that guide a leader's ethical and business decisions. When asked to compose a list of their organization's values, leaders typically mention integrity, quality, customer satisfaction, and enhanced shareholder value. While laudable, which of these would a successful company *not* value, since success demands each of them? A list of ideals *any* organization would embrace doesn't really distinguish a success-driven company from any other, and it doesn't get at the core of what might compromise a particular entity's success. Our Tolstoy fan, Jared Diamond noted, "Only a small percentage of wild mammal species ended up in happy marriages with humans."[1] We can make the same observation about organizations: Successful organizations seem all alike; each unsuccessful one fails in its own way.

Excellence demands that beliefs address the tempests that can trigger failure and provide a compass for navigating uncharted seas, even at high cost. Instead of writing laudable values on a plaque in the foyer, successful leaders *live* their corporate beliefs and expect others to do the same since these beliefs serve as criteria for making business decisions.

Actions—the tough calls involved in running any organization—don't speak louder than words. Frequently, "actions" don't even whisper because they take place between the two ears of senior leaders. However, most people don't consider decision making the most important action leaders take. Decisions—good, bad, seen, or unseen—serve as the link between the leader's beliefs and the results the organization will enjoy or rue. When we trace tragedy and regret back to their roots, we find ourselves lamenting a bad decision, or noticing, in retrospect, a decision a leader didn't even realize he or she made or failed to make. When leaders create an environment where words and actions operate in harmony, however, an almost magical alchemy takes place.

Think of tough calls the way you might imagine ancient alchemy. Alchemy, the medieval forerunner of chemistry, addressed the transformation of matter—attempts to convert base metals into gold by using the Philosopher's Stone or efforts to confer youth and longevity through the Elixir of Life. Alchemy involved liberating parts of the cosmos from temporal existence and achieving perfection—gold for metals and longevity, immortality, and redemption for people.

In organizations, alchemy involves transforming the status quo (the base metals) into the golden ideas of improvement—not just different ideas but better ones. From this change comes innovation, which stands squarely at the heart of organizational learning—with rigidity, caution, and fear as its arch enemies. Fear causes us to build silos that serve as our fortresses. When we fear, we go into protection mode and become risk-averse.

The term "learning culture" presents yet another paradox. Culture acts as a stabilizer—a traditional force, a way of making things predictable. How then, by its very nature, can culture become action-oriented, adoptive, and innovative? How can a leader stimulate and stabilize, at the same time prompting both perpetual learning and change? Maybe the answer lies in perpetual *forgetting*.

An action-oriented environment must contain core shared assumptions that the appropriate way for an organization to improve involves proactive problem-solving, learning from mistakes, and effective decision making about what needs to change. If leaders reflect fatalistic assumptions of passive acceptance, learning becomes more and more difficult as the rate of change in the environment increases. If leaders accept the "we've always done it that way" argument, their beliefs doom the organization to mediocrity. If they could forget for a moment how they've "always done things around here," they could position themselves to take a risk and create an opportunity.

Therefore, leaders must ultimately make the *process* of learning and action—not any given solution to any specific problem—part of the corporate ecosystem. As the problems you encounter change, so will your learning methods. In successful organizations, leaders don't imagine that truth resides in any one source (themselves) or method. Rather, they find truth in experienced practitioners in whom they place their trust, and they expect, experiment with, and experience errors until they find a better solution. They create calculated risks and then give others permission to take them, even when taking the risk might engender failure.

Leaders of the best organizations *expect* failure. They realize that if failure doesn't happen, people haven't pushed hard enough. They refuse to settle for mediocrity in themselves, in their direct reports, in the company's products and services, in customer loyalty, or in financial gain. They set a course for excellence and embrace Dwight D. Eisenhower's ideology: "In battle, our plans may be useless, but the processes indispensable." Successful leaders like Eisenhower see the irrefutable links among planning, learning, decision making, action, and success.

In a constant effort to improve, these leaders make knowledge digestible; they understand that if people can use information quickly and easily, they'll internalize it. They identify sources of innovation and replicate them—continually deconstructing success to understand better how to repeat it or amplify it.

They understand *why* they've had great success, not just *that* they've had it. Additionally, they find out what they and others can do to identify what has to happen to drive the organization to a higher level—not just more volume but more profit. They also eagerly examine failure and cause/effect relationships—not to assign blame but to learn and grow.

Why Believe the Opposite of What You Believe?

Different people define the words "values" and "beliefs" differently, synonymously, and indiscriminately. Traditionally we've thought of values as those things we hold in esteem—a principle, standard, or measure of importance. We form beliefs—acceptance of the truth or actuality of something—based on these values. For this discussion, I will use "belief" to describe something a leader or organizational group believes or accepts as true—convictions that reflect their values and attitudes.

If, therefore, someone has gone to the trouble of developing and examining his or her values and beliefs, why should that person question the opposite of that? Several years ago I asked John that same question.

John inherited a profitable family-owned business that prided itself on quality, service, and integrity. He hired only the best available talent and hired me to make sure he achieved that goal. We worked together successfully over a period until we hit a snag: He simply couldn't find a star performer for a key position. He finally discovered Thomas, a highly skilled professional with the requisite experience and an impressive track record for achieving goals. I felt delighted to call John with the good news that finally we had struck gold.

John seemed lukewarm on the idea of offering Thomas the job, so I did what he hired me to do. I questioned his reluctance. As John explained, Thomas was openly gay, and if Thomas brought his partner to the Christmas party, John's wife "would flip." I suggested they could avoid this situation in one of three ways: by not having a Christmas party, by not having an open Christmas party, or by John suggesting to his wife that *she* not attend. Any seemed a more reasonable solution than John's passing on this extraordinary candidate. John still seemed reluctant.

Then he disclosed that for religious reasons he didn't think he should hire a gay person because "it's just not right." "It" remained a vague pronoun throughout the exchange, but I inferred "it" meant Thomas being gay, not the act of offering a qualified person a job.

Clients hire me to help them with critical decisions, so I felt ethically responsible to help John make this one. If he passed on this exceptional candidate, who knew how long we'd have to wait to find another? And what consequences would the company suffer in the meantime? I posed these questions, but John wasn't convinced he should offer Thomas the job.

Then I reframed. I asked John if he should believe the opposite of what he believed. What did he consider his *primary* responsibility? Should he believe his primary responsibility centers on safeguarding the success of the company, or should he focus on the personal lifestyles of his employees? He admitted that until then, he hadn't really involved himself in the personal lives of his employees and that he knew a couple who had done things he didn't agree with, like having affairs and getting into deep credit-card debt. John didn't abandon his religious beliefs, but together we reframed them. He realized that hiring a gay person didn't imply anything other than his duty to hire the best person for the job.

Reframing helps us forget long-held assumptions and abandon conventional mindsets, but it does something else, too. It frees us to discard the fear-driven, deficiency, scarcity mentality that holds us captive. Until and unless a situation like John's presents itself, we may not even realize we've established a fear mindset. If we can spot the signs, however, we can decide to think of things differently, to think the opposite of what we've always thought. These *Fear Factors* indicate you might need to do that.

Fear Factors

- The inability to celebrate and deconstruct success, to understand not just *that* you've succeeded but to understand exactly *how* and *why* you did.
- A constant need for perfection and more information, even about noncritical issues.
- Concentrating on cutting expenses—layoffs, plant closings, and outsourcing—versus growth.
- Tolerating mediocre performers because "we can't afford superstars."
- Viewing employees as necessary costs, not valued assets.
- A reluctance to develop top performers because they may take their new skills to the competition or, worse yet, they may challenge someone's position in the company.
- An inability or unwillingness to learn and bounce back from failures.
- Lack of clarity about the future.
- Indecision, analysis paralysis, and finger pointing.
- Taking low-margin work to avoid "leaving money on the table."
- Vacillating when an opportunity presents itself, causing a loss of momentum.

- Little investment in improvement.
- A tendency to gloss over conflict, even when you know you're right.
- Feeling overwhelmed, not in control, low energy, no joy.

Advancements in technology—developments that were meant to placate fears—have actually created more problems. A surfeit of information has changed the way we think—and not always for the better. Even though we now better understand how this phenomenon has occurred, it has crept up on us for a long time.

In the 17th century, Gottfried Wilhelm Leibniz, the inventor of calculus, bemoaned the "horrible mass of books which keeps on growing," and 18th-century English poet Alexander Pope warned of "a deluge of authors covering the land." Both considered the consequences of so much data emotional and psychological—anxiety about one's inability to absorb even a small fraction of what's available. They were right then, and the lessons hold true today.

Decision-making science tells us that too much information can lead to choices people regret because our unconscious fears guide our selections—a conundrum that becomes evermore difficult when information never stops arriving. For example, during the BP oil spill of 2010, the worst in U.S. history, Coast Guard Admiral Thad Allen, the incident commander, estimated that he received 300 to 400 *pages* of emails, texts, and messages every day. We will never know whether less information would have allowed officials to figure out sooner how to cap the well, but Allen admitted to reporters that the torrent of data might have contributed to the mistake of failing immediately to close off air space above the gulf—a situation that led to eight near midair collisions.

As Allen learned, every piece of incoming information presents a choice about what to do: pay attention, react, ignore, or prioritize. When people face a plethora of options, however, too often they opt to make no decision at all. We think we want all available data, but frequently an overabundance of information leaves us feeling we have fewer options—and we feel less satisfied with the choices we make. Our fear of criticism or loss of control causes the proliferation of choices to create paralysis when the stakes are high and the information complex.

I often advise clients "perfection is the enemy of success." I'll add here that fear provides an archenemy—a more formidable, insidious opponent that will cripple a leader's personal success, and, eventually, the organization's future. Sometimes we have no interest in believing the opposite of what we believe, nor should we. But when fear drives this conclusion, we do well when we become aware of the driving force behind our reluctance to change beliefs, which needs to precede changing our minds.

Change Your Mind; Boost Your Bottom Line

Frequently, a fear mindset prevents us from killing our sacred cows: fear of rejection, fear of failure, fear of losing control, and even fear of unpleasantness. These fears interfere with learning—causing a defensive reaction that puts the focus on others, not on the person who needs or wants to change. Even when people think they need to change, they prevent the requisite learning by allowing fear to intervene.

When we silence the fears in our heads, we clear the way for more dispassionate, rational thinking. That allows us to shift from a scarcity mentality (there will never be enough) to one of fortitude (I have plenty, or at least enough) to be successful/happy/respected/financially stable. A mindset shift leads to better calls, but it starts with replacing fear with fortitude.

Fortitude Factors

- A refusal to second-guess tough calls
  Psychologists tell us that feeling guilt separates the normal among us from the sociopathic. But that conclusion doesn't explain the debilitating effect guilt—or fear of guilt—can play in preventing us from making difficult decisions. Guilt and its unattractive companion worry are the two most useless of human emotions. Guilt attempts to change the past, while worry serves as the futile effort to change the future. Successful leaders learn not to blame themselves or others for failures—to accept them as a valuable way to learn and grow.

They know that if they don't lose a game once in a while, they're probably not playing in a tough enough league—and they condition themselves not to worry about it.

- Resacralizing

    In his 1971 classic, *The Farther Reaches of Human Nature,* Abraham Maslow introduced the word "resacralizing." He "had to make up these words because the English language is rotten for good people. It has no decent vocabulary for the virtues."[2] Readers understood that desacralizing, often a defense mechanism, involves removing the sacred status or significance from an idea or point of view, even mistrusting the possibility of values and virtues. Resacralizing doesn't *defend* the sacred; it demands the courage to rediscover value. Leaders who resacralize trust their own voices, take responsibility, and work hard to determine what's right, not just what's right now.

- A Quest for self-actualization—the realization or fulfillment of one's talents and potentialities—not a goal to overcome the competition

    Allowing competitors, customers, or employees to draw the map of one's life positions leaders to react in fear when they should proactively create the playing field. Once people understand their strengths and ways to leverage them, however, they enter the more promising, more profitable arena of self-competition. In order words, as fear of failure and outside forces disappear, the self-actualized want to create more happiness, satisfaction, and fulfillment than they already have.

- Originality

    Imitation demands no special set of skills. Anyone can emulate, duplicate, or replicate. Innovation and uniqueness, on the other hand, require the courage to go where no one has gone before, to explore the new frontier, to discover what *can* be, not just what has always been. *Unoriginality* not only doesn't provide the safety net we crave, it leads us to where we were, not to where we need to go.

- You'll Figure It Out

  The boldest leaders I've worked with haven't expressed much interest in following the pack. Instead, they want to set the course with original thinking, which often means thinking on their feet. The ability to get to the core of complex, unfamiliar problems, zero in on the critical few factors, and quickly formulate solutions separates leaders of successful organizations from the "also rans."

  At 40, Rick, the president of a construction company, faced the most complicated decisions of his professional life. The owners of a major construction project simply wouldn't reason. They expected him and his company to absorb cost overruns; they showed no willingness to help complete the project within a firm deadline. Rick lost sleep the first few times he encountered these never-before-seen problems. He lost sleep because the consequences loomed large and real. He lost sleep until he figured out that he *always* figures it out, and that he would figure it out the next time too.

  When people have a track record for figuring things out, as Rick did, they build confidence and optimism. They believe they can and will figure things out the next time they face the dragon. They don't expect to slay the dragon *every* time, but they have the confidence that they will emerge victorious more often than not, and the good guys will eventually win.

- Get help

  Most successful leaders realize what got them *here* won't get them *there*, wherever the next "there" happens to be. Yet, overusing a strength to the point that it becomes a weakness has reached epidemic proportion. Leaders who have moved up the corporate ladder relied on their independence to help them achieve. But at the upper echelons of the organization, they discover that others expect and demand teamwork. The often feel as though someone changed the rules in the seventh inning of the game.

  The hard-charging, self-reliant, win-at-all-cost mindset spurs a fear-driven manager to become a leader, but this same mindset can cripple the same person who aspires to reach higher. It's getting lonelier at the top, so leaders who seek to improve must acquire knowledge, embrace behavior change, and develop skills continuously. Sometimes these leaders need help, so they get it from people who have the expertise to give it and the ability to build a relationship in which the leader can trust the advice.

- Eschewing unsolicited feedback
  Seeking advice and counsel takes a certain degree of courage; rejecting unsolicited feedback takes even more fortitude and self-awareness. People with a strong commitment to self-improvement often eagerly and misguidedly take what they can get in terms of advice, analysis, and assessment. They overlook the fact that, more often than not, the feedback says more about the need for the giver to *say* it than the receiver to *hear* it.

  Over the years, self-proclaimed experts have approached me and my fellow professional speakers right after we leave the stage to ask, "Can I give you some feedback?" For years I responded, "Of course." Now, I simply say, "No thank you." Putting aside the need to seem overly responsive or the desire to be universally liked requires fortitude; patiently allowing someone to abuse the moment does not.

- A Willingness to deconstruct success
  Having coached hundreds of leaders for thousands of hours, I can tell you unequivocally most people want to talk about their weaknesses more than they do their successes. When I open a feedback session with, "Do you have any questions before we get started?" 9.5 times out of 10 the person says, "Yes. Tell me about my weaknesses, and suggest what I can do about them." My response stays the same, no matter how many times I hear this: "You aren't sitting here getting ready for promotion because of your weaknesses. I only work with high potentials, and you're on the road to promotion, so wouldn't it make better sense to spend our time talking about how to leverage your *strengths*?" This usually brings a look of stunned disbelief, which every coach relishes.

Quashing fear moves the needle on self-improvement and makes tough calls easier, but no one should confuse the absence of fear with fortitude. Grit, pluck, determination, and valor define fortitude—with a little audacity thrown in to help people decide what they believe then having the courage to act on those beliefs. Although attributed to many, most believe Winston Churchill pointed out that "failure is seldom fatal, and success never final—it's courage that counts."

The Differences Between Espoused Beliefs and Operating Beliefs

When he said, "What you are speaks so loudly I can't hear what you say," Ralph Waldo Emerson captured the essence of what separates espoused beliefs (what we say we believe) from operating beliefs (the way we do things around here). But Emerson's observation omitted some other factors that influence beliefs, such as habits, mental models, traditions—or the way we've *always* done things around here.

Espoused beliefs start with an individual's perception of right and wrong—someone's sense of what *ought* to be as opposed to what *is*. When outcomes prove the individual right, and others observe this, they create shared beliefs or shared assumptions that the same course of action will work into the future.

For example, the leader of a sales group advocates a team approach to sales. She revamps the compensation package to reward team behavior. Then everyone sees sales soar. The leader's espoused value of the importance of teamwork quickly turns to a shared assumption that teams, rather than individuals, should work to increase business. Over time, as newcomers adopt a team approach, the espoused value gradually morphs into an operating belief—but only if the approach continues to meet sales demands. A transformation occurs; habits form; mindsets evolve, all giving birth to a tradition . . . a track record.

When the gap between the two—what you merely say and what you really do—narrows, tough decisions become easier because leaders have learned to make their decisions based on their core values—the intersection of what we believe and how we behave. But it doesn't always work that way. One large hospital's espoused belief did not intersect with their operating beliefs—the way they did things.

Espoused Belief

People Above All: Treating those we serve with compassion, dignity, and respect.

Operating Belief

This "people above all else" orientation does not extend to managers in the company who cannot replace substandard employees with competent ones. HR runs the show at this hospital and has made both hiring stars and firing incompetents nearly impossible.

Espoused Belief

Excellence: Acting with integrity and striving for the highest quality care and service.

Operating Belief

The hospital allows itself to lose millions of dollars a year due to improper coding of services, low productivity, and low morale. Excellent employees become frustrated and leave as soon as a position opens in another hospital. The malcontents, however, *never* leave because they know a good deal when they see it, and the hospital's unwillingness to strive for quality provides fertile ground for their discontent to grow.

Espoused Belief

Results: Exceeding the expectations of those we serve and those we set for ourselves.

Operating Belief

The expectations of internal customers don't matter. Departments can operate in silos and don't have to rely on each other. Expectations don't exist or haven't been communicated consistently. Instead, they have "coaching," "advanced coaching," "reminders," and even "advanced reminders."

As often happens, the gaps between the espoused beliefs and operating beliefs did not become apparent until the hospital launched a major acquisition. Then, things started to change rapidly. At no time did anyone seem to detect the inconsistencies, however. The espoused beliefs, therefore, represented espoused *aspirations* more than true beliefs. The hospital chain continues to struggle, with the added complexity of integration after an acquisition.

Another client experienced a great deal of unexplained turnover over the course of several years. The boutique firm had contracted with me to help them hire more efficiently and effectively. I couldn't understand why all the high potentials I recommended did not stay very long. They paid a competitive, though not generous, salary, but I suspected money was not the culprit. They also created an attractive work environment with reasonable work rules, but people continued to leave at alarming rates—just about the time they had completed training in the company's processes and procedures. The turnover and costs of hiring new people mounted up, but the cause remained elusive.

During our engagement, I happened to visit their offices on Halloween and had a conversation with one of the employees, Mary, about her plans for the evening. As a new grandmother, Mary would have the chance to see her grandson in a costume for the first time. She beamed with excitement.

The next day I asked her how she had enjoyed her first Halloween with her new grandson. Fighting tears, she confided her boss had dumped a huge amount of work on her desk at the close of the day, and she had to stay late to finish it. Her boss, who notoriously left things until the last minute and never seemed to make a deadline, knew of Mary's plans but showed no empathy for her. Ironically, this firm specialized in helping clients develop people skills—that stood as their espoused mission—but they neglected to treat their own employees with empathy and respect. Soon, more reasons for the high turnover surfaced, and it became apparent that you could drive a truck through the space between what the company claimed to believe and how they behaved with their own employees.

Because the human mind craves stability, when people become aware of the disparities between stated beliefs and observed behavior, they feel more motivated to reduce the differences, to be more consistent, to reduce dissonance. They learn to reflect critically on their behavior, identify the ways they often inadvertently contribute to their own problems, and then they change their actions. Theoretically, that's how it would happen.

In reality, here's what happens. Since successful executives succeed and rarely fail, they seldom create the opportunities to learn from failure. However, failure is instructive, and smart people learn more from their failures than they do from their successes. Consequently, when leaders cleave to stability when they really need to welcome change, their ability to learn falters precisely at the moment they need learning and growth most, which makes them defensive and further limits their ability to learn from a mistake. The owners of the firm where Mary worked wanted to retain top talent, but they wouldn't or didn't look at their own behavior or that of their senior leaders as causes. Consequently, nothing changed; they continue to struggle, and the revolving door at the front of their building continues to spin faster than ever.

People who refuse to learn design their actions according to one of four basic beliefs, which correspond with the four major categories of fear:

1. I want to be liked.
2. I need to be in control.
3. I need to be "right."
4. I can't experience unpleasantness (guilt, shame, embarrassment, vulnerability).

Espoused beliefs predict well enough what people will *say*, but these words may or may not align with what people actually *do* in situations where these beliefs should operate. Insightful leaders kill sacred cows every time they discriminate between congruent and incongruent circumstances. They understand also that they must distinguish rationalizations and aspirations. Nature abhors a vacuum, and so do employees. They don't want large areas of unexplained behavior. They want leaders who understand that the human mind needs cognitive stability—leaders who relieve anxiety and defensiveness. Improvement begins with the leader's self-awareness and self-regulation—which includes, first, an allegiance to stretching, even when it might mean failure—and, then, a commitment to learn from failure when it occurs. It all starts with a "can do" belief.

Forget Self-Esteem; Learn Optimism

Many people now leading major organizations function like victims of the so-called self-esteem movement that began in the 1960s and continues to this day. The movement quickly gained momentum, resulting in a 1990 decision of the California legislature to sponsor a report suggesting that self-esteem be taught in every classroom as a "vaccine" against social ills, such as alcohol abuse, drug addition, suicide, and teen pregnancy.

In 1986, former California state legislator John Vasconcellos established the "Task Force to Promote Self-Esteem and Personal and Social Responsibility." This prompted a three-year, twenty-five-member investigation into the effect self-esteem has on society. The task force's records consist of five and one-half cubic feet of textual material and five cubic feet of audiovisual material covering the years 1987 to 1990.[3] Cartoonist Garry Trudeau lampooned the effort in his *Doonesbury* comic strip, calling it "the embodiment of California wackiness."

Not everyone got the joke. The task force, which operated from 1987 to 1990, was a serious, or at least expensive, enterprise. It looked at the role of self-esteem in various areas, from crime and violence to academic failure and responsible citizenship. The commission's final report, released in 1990, became the best-selling state document of all time, selling 60,000 copies.

Even without finding *causal* links between self-esteem and success, proponents of this movement advocated the demise of IQ testing, tracking in public schools, and class ranking. The movement gave birth to the everybody-gets-a-trophy mindset that society must adopt in order, advocates said, to avoid scarring underperforming children. Without question, a *correlation* between self-esteem and success exists, but no one actually proved *causality*. In other words, people who do well in school, sports, or business often exhibit signs that they possess high self-esteem, but no proof exists that the high self-esteem actually *causes* the success. In fact, evidence exists to the contrary.

In 1996, researcher Roy Baumeister and his colleagues killed this sacred task-force cow in their study of genocidal killers, hit men, gang leaders, and other violent criminals. These researchers found that perpetrators with *unwarranted* high self-esteem became violent—meaning that these reprobates *felt* good about themselves without actually *doing* anything laudable. These findings suggest that if you teach unwarrantedly high self-esteem to children, without demanding praiseworthy behavior in return, confusion ensues. When these children confront the real world, and it tells them they are not as great as they have been taught, they lash out with violence.[4] Is it possible then, that violence stems from the misbegotten notion that valuing how children feel about themselves more highly than how we value how they behave causes problems? Is it also possible that this everybody-gets-a-trophy mindset might also keep leaders from making tough calls? Tough calls become tougher when we confuse reality with what we think *ought* to be.

Putting this confusion to rest does not promote envy or enlarge the number of society's losers. Rather, it provides support for ideas that have shaped past progress—ideas that will aid future advancement so society as a whole wins—in other words, we become better educated, more productive, and healthier.

Americans have stubbornly clung to the myth of egalitarianism—supremacy of the individual average person. We created the everyone-gets-a-trophy culture among our young, then it morphed into Cuckooland, a place where we shield losers who lose based on consequences from thinking they deserve to lose, and suggests we should bar winners who win fairly from feeling confidence and pride.

Organizational success, the economic recovery, and indeed global resurgence, depend on something better—better, not just different. Success depends on a shift back to the notion that self-fulfillment—seductive though it may appear—must march in lockstep with a commitment to achievement.

Let's not totally disregard the importance of self-assuredness. Instead, let's understand it better and dispassionately evaluate the role it plays in engendering success. To start, we need to rediscover the intellectual confidence it takes to sort out and rank competing values. Fairness does not equal equality. Equal opportunity at the starting gun does not and should not guarantee equality at the finish line. Those who run through the tape at the finish line offer our greatest hope for thriving in the new economy.

Dr. Martin Seligman, the vanguard in the arena of positive psychology, pointed out that we have become depressed with a disorder of the "I," meaning we fail in our own eyes relative to the expectations we have for ourselves or that other people have for us. In a society in which individualism has become rampant, people too often believe they are the center of the universe. This dark side of self-esteem, therefore, makes individuals who fail inconsolable, and tough calls feel more threatening.

A second force, which Seligman called the large "we," used to serve as a force to buffer failure. When our grandparents failed, they had comfortable spiritual furniture to rest on—a safe place to land. They had their relationships with God, with a nation, with communities, and with a large extended family. Our faith in religions, community, the nation, and each other has all eroded in the past 40 years. The spiritual furniture we used to sit on has become threadbare, and the self-esteem movement has not helped us recover what we've lost.[5]

I'll call what we've lost "self-respect." When we have feelings of self-worth, not just entitlement, we can resist feelings of inadequacy and the imposter syndrome that makes us fear we'll be identified and humiliated—or fired. The greatest obstacle so many of my clients face involves the voice in their heads that whispers—and sometimes shouts—words of discouragement. The reason? So many at the top don't solicit objective feedback from trusted advisers—people who have no other agenda than helping them improve. They get confused and either don't make the tough calls or make them only to rue them.

Leaders of every stripe must look for and welcome objective data about their talents, but too few do. Yet, books like *Now Discover Your Strengths* seem never to leave the bestseller list. We truly seem to want to move forward, to feel better about ourselves, and to enjoy more success, but too often we don't recognize that optimism, rather than exaggerated self-esteem, which I'll call arrogance, holds the key. When we learn optimism, we happily face our challenges instead of viewing each day as a slow crawl through enemy territory. Eisenhower seemed to figure this out more than 70 years before Rick did.

On June 6, 1944, Allied Expeditionary Force Supreme Commander Dwight D. Eisenhower undertook the largest air, land, and sea operation before or since 1944. The Invasion of Normandy established Western Allied forces through Operation Overlord—a decisive battle of epic scope that foreshadowed the end of Hitler's dream of Nazi domination. This largest of amphibious invasions included more than 5,000 ships, 11,000 airplanes, and 150,000 military members. Of these 150,000, more than 100,000 men made it ashore and changed the course of history, even though they suffered nearly 10,000 casualties and 4,000 deaths.

Eisenhower knew that only 10 days during that month would be suitable for launching the operation. They needed a day near a full moon to illuminate navigational landmarks for the aircraft crews. They needed the spring tide to expose defensive obstacles placed in the surf by the Germans. They faced nearly insurmountable odds: weather conditions threatened the operation; the invasion would require moving forces 100 miles across the English Channel; less than 15 percent of Allied forces had ever seen combat; and they faced the weapon-and-tank-superior German army commanded by Rommel, one of the most brilliant generals in history.

Eisenhower had tentatively selected June 5 as the date for the landing, but on June 4, wind, high seas, and low clouds thwarted his plans. Another full moon would not occur for a month, and returning troops to their embarkation camps would be nearly impossible due to the sheer numbers of them already in position. The weather forecast implied but did not guarantee a brief improvement for June 6, so Eisenhower launched.

What equipped the 53-year-old Eisenhower to make one of the toughest calls in history? Certainly, he had attended West Point, but while there, he achieved only average academic performance and less than stellar discipline ratings. He had enjoyed a long career in the army and had served during World War I but without leaving the shores of America, a fact rival generals such as Montgomery used to denigrate Eisenhower. So, while he generally embodied all of the four constructs needed for tough calls—moral gyroscope, fortitude, experience, and judgment—he needed one more attribute to help him make this pivotal call: the confidence that he could. This self-assuredness comes from the magical alchemy that converted his basic traits into golden decisions. Optimism served as the Philosopher's Stone that allowed the transformation.

Eisenhower exuded optimism—not a cockeyed, Pollyanna view of the world but an honest-to-goodness belief that he could overcome obstacles and turn challenges into victories. How did he develop this attitude?

Probably from irrefutable evidence that he always *had* overcome obstacles. When facing yet *another* obstacle in Normandy, he had an established belief that they could accomplish something that had never been done before—the "I'll figure it out attitude" that makes all the difference.

Optimists don't deny reality or have a less than pragmatic approach to decision making, but they don't fall into the pessimism trap either. An optimist doesn't ignore chest pains and hope for the best, but neither does he feel helpless during the experience. He calls 911 and takes the necessary precautions to control what he can control. He hasn't learned helplessness, so he doesn't allow himself to feel victimized. He feels empowered to do what he knows to do to mitigate a bad situation.

Pessimists tend to believe that bad events will last a long time and undermine everything else, and the pessimist is somehow to blame for them. I have often concluded that pessimists feel a sense of control over the future by worrying and ruing a future state—as though their fretting will somehow appease the gods and avoid the bad outcome. Pessimism also provides an excuse: "I might as well give up since nothing I do will make a difference anyway."

In any discussion of optimism, I'm reminded of the comments of one of my Vietnam POW participants. During an interview for my research, one of the POWs explained how the POWs had distinguished between an optimist and a pessimist: The pessimist believed they would all be killed in Vietnam and buried in Vietnam. The optimist believed they'd be killed in Vietnam, but their bodies would be shipped home. Of course, this also illustrates the valuable role humor plays in coping with a situation over which a person has no control.

Optimists, even when confronted with an identical bad event, think of things in the opposite way. They see defeats as temporary and surmountable—chances to meet a challenge and to try harder. People learn helplessness and pessimism, so it stands to reason they can learn optimism too. But often they need help to reframe their thinking.

One of the techniques I use with clients involves a close examination of what has caused their success. Instead of focusing on failures, mistakes, and weaknesses, I point out that, since I only work with top performers in successful companies, I wouldn't be working with them if they weren't successful. How do we work together?

- We deconstruct success. By asking people what they have achieved, we can map out the reasons for success and set a plan for replicating the success. Even though they want to explain and explore the aspects of the project or initiative that *didn't* work, by gently pulling them back to objective reality, we can see what has to happen in the future for them to enjoy success similar to their past achievements.
- We focus on success, not perfection. Often people feel helpless and hopeless when they realize, no matter what they do, they can't ever achieve perfection. They can achieve accuracy, precision, excellence, and triumph, but human endeavors won't ever be perfect. Once a person accepts that reality, the work becomes more manageable and success more likely.
- We look at the evidence. Often we have automatic thoughts about ourselves that don't serve us well. That is, we fall into the trap of believing what we once or have always told ourselves: "I'm not good with numbers," "I am not high energy," or the worst one, "I don't deserve success." With help, we can learn to stand back and look at things through a different lens, one that teaches us that we have every reason to be optimistic. Rick learned to tell himself he would "figure it out" because the evidence indicated that he always *had*, so he benefited from realizing he always *can*.
- We learn new coping skills. Just as the POWs discovered the value of using humor to distract them from harsh realities, we can develop techniques to rise above negative, self-defeating thoughts. Often this involves including a trusted adviser in our ruminations and knowing our limitations for handling setbacks alone.

If Eisenhower had lacked any of the four basics for making tough calls, we have to wonder whether he could have made the complicated decision to launch Operation Overlord—the Great Crusade—but he didn't. He had all four and the added dimension of optimism. The eyes of the world were upon him, and the prayers of liberty-loving people everywhere marched with him.

Conclusion

We venerate our sacred cows, traditions, and conventional approaches because they make us feel secure. But like all emotional security blankets, they unravel, and their usefulness fades. When we replace emotional responses with new attitudes and cognitive skills, and we challenge ourselves to take risks, reframe, and live well-thought-out beliefs instead of clinging to what we've always done, we open the door for new opportunities and optimism. Making tough calls may involve the demise of some bovines, but it might also mean seeing what remains to be seen. In the words of Jimmy Buffet:

> Yesterday's over my shoulder, so I can't look back for too long.
>
> There's just too much to see waiting in front of me, and I know I can't go wrong
>
> With these changes in latitudes, changes in attitudes, nothing remains quite the same. With all of our running and all of our cunning, if we couldn't laugh, we would all go insane.

CHAPTER 3

Become the Company That Could Put You Out of Business

If you visit Dunvegan Castle on the Isle of Skye in Scotland, you will see a yellow silk flag encased in glass, reputed to have originated in the Far East, possibly brought to Scotland by the Crusaders . . . or . . . maybe Vikings from Norway brought it. Or, it's a saint's relic. The Clan McLeod knows the real story.

Centuries ago, the fourth Chief of the Clan McLeod, Laird Lain Ciar, and a beautiful fairy princess fell in love. Her father allowed the marriage on the condition that she would return to the Land of the Fairies after one year. Lady McLeod gave the clan chief a beautiful baby boy, whom she agreed to leave with her husband, asking only that the baby *never* be left alone or crying.

For months the Laird grieved the loss of his wife until his kinsmen decided to throw a great feast to cheer him up. The revelry did raise his spirits, but it also distracted the child's nursemaid, who left him unattended as she looked in on the festivities.

The baby awakened, but no one heard him cry—no one *except* his mother in the Land of the Fairies. When the Laird realized the nursemaid had left his son alone, he dashed from the banquet hall to the nursery to find his wife kissing the baby as she wrapped him in a yellow shawl, leaving the baby once more in his father's care as she vanished before their eyes.

Once grown and having realized the mystical nature of his wrap, the boy assured his father that the shawl held mystical powers, ones that would protect his clan even in the direst circumstances. Consequently, through the centuries, the clan has relied on the flag for its legendary protection. Little remains of it, however, because during the Second World

War, young McLeod RAF pilots carried small scraps of it in their wallets as they went into battle. Not one McLeod man was shot down in the entire war—not one. Did the fairy flag save them? If they *believed* it did, it probably did. That's the nature of mysticism.

The McLeods have told the story of the flag through the centuries, relying on legends to help each new generation understand what it means to belong to the clan—the first powerhouse. Most modern organizations can trace their origins and legends back decades, not centuries. But most of the successful organizations that have survived and thrived in a tough economy embody lessons that have endured through the ages.

The company that could put you out of business hires top performers—those who want to belong to a clan they respect, one that will protect them in dire circumstances, and one to whom they proudly give their allegiance. Arguably, evident characteristics like strong strategic focus, effective leadership, and shared values form the foundation of any successful organization, but that doesn't tell the whole story. Something even more abstract plays a role too.

Many of the important aspects of an organizational powerhouse never make their way to the policy manuals, forecasted revenues, or written summaries. Like the proud traditions of a clan, people pass the stories from generation to generation or cubicle to cubicle. Leaders influence both the stories and the people through acts of courage, but ultimately day-to-day tough calls define how the tartan plaid of an organization will weave themselves together.

Coach the Clever People in Your Clan

The word *clan* derives from the Gaelic word *clanna*, meaning children or offspring, which originally implied members shared a common ancestor. However, through the centuries, people started to regard clans not only as family members but also as kinship groups that provided a sense of shared identity—a distinction others could see and recognize by tartan patterns members often incorporated into kilts and other clothing. Many clansmen, although not related to the chief, took the chief's surname as their own to show solidarity—a unity that allowed them basic protection and much-needed sustenance.

Although needs have changed through the centuries, and we no longer rely on our employers to provide protection against foreign enemies, many of the proud traditions of the clans live on. Some companies, like airlines, require employees to wear uniforms to distinguish them from employees of competing airlines, and we continue to depend on employers for sustenance in the form of paychecks. We also continue to need to replace current members of our groups with new members and to add members and equip leaders as the company grows and expands. But now most successful companies realize they can't depend on their current and legendary approaches to attract new employees. Rather, they need a new way to draw people—especially star-quality clan-worthy people—into the circle. They realize they need to become magnets for the talent they want.

The McLeods believe they have the fairies looking after them, but you may need a more tangible strategy—one that starts with inviting the best people into your clan. When you combine the best allies with a brave approach to your business, you'll succeed no matter what economic enemies mount a battle against you.

If you played sports in school, did the coach play everyone equally? Create an egalitarian form of governance in which each person had a say? Or, did the stars, the ones who had the innate athletic ability and drive to put those skills into action, receive a disproportionate amount of playing time and the coach's attention? If you won many games, I suspect the second scenario—and a series of daily tough calls on the coach's part.

Fairness demands each person receives an equal opportunity to succeed, not equal treatment along the way. If your high potentials show a willingness to work extra hours, take additional training, and pursue advanced degrees, why shouldn't you reward them? As your athletic coaches understood, so you need to understand. Only by grooming the top 20 percent of your talent will you ultimately win the war for talent. Certainly, compensate them monetarily, but also reward them with the best and the most valuable and least expensive prize of all—your mentoring.

Even though we see the value of coaching the stars in sports arenas, in organizations, we tend to resist this reality. We address nonproductive behavior and underachievers—ignoring the stellar performance of the few but mighty. When we do this, stars vote with their feet by walking out the doors—right through the door of your competitors. "A" players want to play on winning teams, and they don't suffer "C" and "D" players too long or too much. "A" players demand your attention, but giving it to them won't always prove easy.

One of the most challenging issues you'll face, in fact, will be coaching high potentials. As people near peak performance, tasks become mundane, problems less interesting, and opportunities less fascinating. The adrenaline wanes. Stars start to experience discontent and wonder what happened to the excitement. You may see less enthusiasm and a subtle loss of edge.

Most leaders don't know how to develop clever people, even if they themselves qualify as stars. How can you change that?

- You can't fool clevers with titles, even though they appreciate ones that mean something. Provide ever-changing, challenging work, and give them real authority to make a difference.
- Hire other "A" players to support their teams. Make your organization a place where the clever choose to work, and your stars will become your best magnets for other top performers.
- Celebrate innovation and experimentation, even when that allows or leads to an occasional failure. Clever people like to create. Give them that chance.
- They know their worth, so compensate them fairly. Even though star performers don't usually count compensation among their reasons for taking or leaving a job, they do have a sense of fair play and will expect you to reward them for being the best.
- Top performers don't respond well to autocratic leadership. Nor do they appreciate laissez-faire leadership. They want direction but in the form of democratic guidance, not an absence of direction.
- Try to micromanage a star just a little, and you will lose that person.
- "A" players want access—to you, your top clients, investors, and anyone else important to the organization.

- Give genuine, meaningful accolades. Star performers require praise, but unless you offer it sincerely and specifically, they will dismiss it.
- Encourage the best and brightest to lead with strategy, not tactics. Often, in fact, they lack strong detail orientation and need others to keep them on track.

Don't Do Well What You Shouldn't Do in the First Place

Not everyone agrees that organizational success starts with leaders and their pivotal decisions. Instead, leaders frequently allow this force they call "culture" to dwell and even to run amok in the arena of the unconscious—which makes culture both powerful and dangerous—and prevent the creation of a powerhouse. Often these leaders aren't aware of their own biases until and unless someone challenges them. Sometimes this challenge comes from an external adviser or acquiring company, but more often it comes from customers or from the competition.

When things work, and the future promises more of the same, people lack the motivation to talk about or think about change. However, history has taught us that a once-formidable powerhouse can lose its footing in its industry with one significant slip. Then the question becomes, "What will we have to do to keep ahead of the competition?" or "What's the competition's winning move now and in the future?" Since we don't know what twists and turns lie ahead, we rely on current evidence to make decisions about change.

Creating or changing organizations doesn't happen easily or automatically—at least not successfully. Instead, when leaders realize they want to transform the environment of their organizations—often after a crisis, change of leadership, or acquisition, they have three choices:

1. Destroy major elements of the existing culture, which usually means getting rid of key decisions makers.
2. Generally accept the existing environment but make modifications when evidence suggests they should.
3. Change.

The first option involves a complete overhaul—to dismantle what exists, even before you know what future options might look like. This sort of change often accompanies a merger or acquisition. But even when mergers and acquisitions occur, the acquiring company typically saw enough value in the other company to want to buy it, so completely destroying it makes no sense. Macy's acquisition of Marshall Field's offers an exception.

Even though the leadership at Macy's kept the Chicago retailer in its original buildings, and the stores remained department stores, decision makers changed the name of the stores, the merchandise they sold, and their position in the market. As often happens, the stores lost key customers and the loyalty of the Chicago market—a previously faithful clientele.

Former Assistant to the President for Communication, David Gergen, recalled that President Regan once announced, "We didn't come here to fiddle with the controls. We came to change the direction of the ship." Sound as the commitment was for a president, sometimes companies just need a little fiddling with the controls. In these cases, leaders limit changes to those things that cry out for improvement, not just alternatives that might be better. The third option, true change, happens most successfully when compelling evidence exists that the change will bring innovation, not just differences.

Pros and cons exist for each option. Start by challenging beliefs about the status quo. *Why* do we do what we do? Frequently you'll find no one who can answer that question, except to explain, "Because we've always done it that way" or "Our founder thought that was important, so we carried on after he was gone." Too many leaders have developed contempt for simplicity and structure, often because those in the chain of command have muddied the waters, frequently in defensive moves to justify failures or elevate their own value to the company.

"Culture," the overused buzzword of the financial recovery, has transformed from an ethereal, abstract, otherworldly word to a blunt instrument for finding fault on myriad qualitative matters affecting the organization. No one seems to know what it means, what it looks like, what symptoms indicate it works, or how to measure it. Culture, the new rabbit both leaders and regulators want to chase, jumps from one issue to another before it disappears down a hole, only to resurface with the problems it spawned or ignored while in hiding.

Instead, Create a Powerhouse

Defining the decision dilemma related to the company's environment is the first step. *Measuring* it offers more challenges. We can't measure organizational environments the way we assess chlorine levels in a swimming pool, but if we start with a list of criteria for evaluating the atmosphere around them, we move closer to controlling it. This model shows how organizations evolve:

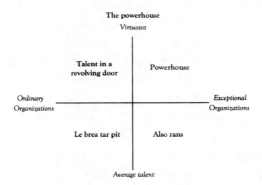

Each quadrant represents the desirable or undesirable ways companies evolve, highlighting the necessity of inexorably linking top talent and organizational success. The *Revolving Door* quadrant represents those companies that have hired and developed top talent but failed to create an environment in which they can do their best work. These kinds of companies stay in business because they routinely recruit and hire the best and brightest in their industries, but then the music stops, and they must start all over.

Leaders in these companies fail to embrace some of the critical elements of the exceptional organization: a clear strategy, a commitment to excellence, and change-oriented culture. While they seem to understand the value of hiring top talent, they persistently tie the hands of those talented recruits. Virtuosos want clear direction, consistency, agility, and a culture built on beliefs they can embrace themselves. Fail to deliver on any one of these requirements, and you essentially install a revolving door that spins your top talent right out into the street.

Ordinary companies that hire average people won't even end up with a mediocre organization, however, because, through the years, these ordinary people gradually turn their environment into a Le Brea Tar Pit—a home for the fossilized, the walking dead, the uninspired, unmotivated, and unseemly who can gradually but capably kill a company.

Nearly as devastating, average team members who enter an exceptional organization can gradually turn the company into an *Also Ran* among competitors. Average talent tends to seek its own level—hiring and promoting people who offer mediocrity that won't threaten anyone in a position of power. Soon, these average players settle for average profits, unexceptional quality, and a tactical, day-by-day approach to work. They don't have a vision because they lack strategic thinking skills to develop one.

What can leaders do to bring about the necessary changes to build a powerhouse—the kind of company that could put them out of business? Start by creating a polarizing effect, removing what you *don't* want and replacing it with what you *do* want.

Many leaders' first impulse compels them to look inward—to do an employee engagement survey, to conduct focus groups, or to seek consensus about some major decision. Measuring things like how often people go to happy hour together or where they rank themselves and others on a happy-to-grumpy scale provides no useful information. Not one shred of evidence exists to indicate that happy employees act more ethically than unhappy ones, but theorists persist in measuring this and other interesting but irrelevant data.

That does not imply an internal focus will offer *no* help. Start any change initiative by examining core values, teamwork, learning capacity, and employee empowerment. And then ask the tough questions:

To what extent do we model our beliefs?
Convey respect for each other?
Foster and reward teamwork?
Work through conflict?
Encourage two-way communication?

Looking inward comes easily to most leaders. Recently a prospective client called to ask whether I could help conduct and interpret an employee engagement survey. Of course, almost anyone can buy and administer that sort of assessment, but I questioned why they would choose that path when I had no idea what objective they had set. The board director who called said they "just want to see how bad things are." I told him things *must* be bad if they want to measure them.

Then I asked what he, the other directors, and the CEO would do with the results of the survey. He didn't know. They had chosen an arbitrary path to an unknown destination. I encouraged him to abandon this idea until we understood and agreed about the results they wanted and the information they lacked. In other words, they wanted to measure the beliefs that were leading to actions and results they didn't want. Not only will this approach *not* build a powerhouse; it will likely put the company in the poorhouse. Although well intended, this firm's leaders got off track and didn't hire me. Their methodology didn't work, and the company continues to struggle. At no point during our discussion did they show openness to examining external forces, like their reputation in the industry, their relationships with investor, or their standing with their customers.

We create the environment of organizations as we go along, sometimes consciously, often unconsciously—but always through decisions. When leaders decide to build a powerhouse of excellence, they start by asking themselves what needs to change and what should stay the same.

Change and improvement should start with a periscope, not a microscope. Looking into the external environment allows decision makers to determine how they should adapt in response to the changes they see in the world: the economy, the industry, the country, and the world. This external focus then allows leaders to examine their mission, strategic direction, and goals in context. Most importantly, it puts the emphasis on the customer.

Customer comments and recommendations should shine the light into the darkness to help influence decisions and results. Companies that ignore the customer's desires find themselves short on customers. That's what decision makers at General Motors did.

General Motors had been a powerhouse on and off since its inception in 1908. Like most other automakers, GM has faced the ups and downs of a troubled industry. GM led global vehicle sales for 77 consecutive years from 1931 through 2007, longer than any other automaker, but then faced bankruptcy in 2009 and a recall scandal in 2014.

A headline in the *Wall Street Journal* on June 6, 2014, read "GM Takes Blame, Vows Culture Shift," once again using that blunt instrument called "culture" to place blame. But what really happened to cause more than 120 deaths? What factors led to the once-powerful GM's decline in status? Let's examine the beliefs and actions that fueled the results.

Beliefs:

- Executives believed they did not need to understand how the company made cars, as evidenced by their failure to recognize that a sudden-shutoff switch qualified as a safety concern, not a customer-convenience issue. Had senior decision makers connected the dots and understood *how* they built cars, they would have recognized the need for an immediate recall, addressing the safety defect before it caused injuries and fatalities.
- U.S. Attorney Anton Valukas concluded that the information about the defect bounced around an astonishing number of committees without anyone making the recall decision—each person apparently believing he or she had neither the responsibility nor the authority to make the tough call.
- CEO Mary Barra described the "GM Nod" that involved meeting participants nodding in agreement that GM *should* take action but no one stepping up to make the decision or take the step.
- Another GM official described the "GM Salute," which involved crossing one's arms while pointing to one's colleagues on the left or right, indicating that the blame or responsibility resides elsewhere.
- Barra also denounced a pattern of incompetence and neglect, pointing out the company's reluctance either to hire top talent or to expect top performance from the talent it had.

Actions:

- Decision making bounced around with no one taking responsibility for the decisions themselves, much less taking the actions they should have taken as a result of them.
- No one connected the dots, which would have allowed leaders to address the safety defect.
- A troubling disavowal of responsibility
- Even though some realized the need in 2013 for the recall, leaders waited with no sense of urgency while they gathered more data and endangered more motorists.

Results:

- Link to more than 120 deaths
- $900 million penalty
- $575 million to settle nearly 1,400 lawsuits
- $625 million to establish a compensation fund for victims
- Irreparable damage to the GM brand

Mary Barra, a GM veteran, inherited the recall crisis shortly after she became CEO in January of 2014. Her promotion coincided with the release of a company-funded report that shone a negative light on the recall disgrace and a 315-page report by former U.S. Attorney Anton Valukas that outlined the devastating consequences. Berra's vow to shift the culture that led to these consequences represented an important first step, but actually making that shift won't happen until and unless she, other leaders, and board directors understand the factors that threatened GM's status as a powerhouse in the first place.

They've made a start by choosing the first of the aforementioned three options for change: destroying elements of the existing culture, which, in this case, involved firing 15 employees—more than half of them executives—for misconduct or failure to respond properly. The company also fired lawyers and officials responsible for safety. But Barra won't truly change anything significant as long as she blames *patterns* of incompetence and neglect and not *specific people* and their bad decisions. The solution is neither abstract nor otherworldly. Improvement will occur only when leaders change the beliefs that led to the decisions that caused the consequences.

Knowing what to look for and then making decisions to act on the information can turn things around, however. Ideas—not style—define leadership, which involves tying those ideas to core beliefs, making the right decisions, and expecting dramatic results. Only when leaders understand this new paradigm will they be able to raise the BAR and initiate major strategic and tactical change programs that will position their organizations for success.

Become Repulsive on Purpose

In the realm of tough calls, being repulsive does not mean being nauseating or vile. Rather, it means rejecting easy fixes and rebuffing bad ideas, even when you couch them in good intentions. It means resisting the comfort that the sacred cows promise and snubbing the much-lauded relief of problem-solving when the situation demands innovation. Repulsion also involves rejecting interference from functions that should offer support but that too often operate as "business prevention units" (HR, legal, compliance, finance, IT).

Sometimes bad ideas start as good intentions—not frequently, but sometimes. In these situations, leaders fail to distinguish motive from consequences. Sometimes a well-intended person offers a solution that is shortsighted or misguided, but it comes from the heart or some other good place, so the decision maker does not anticipate repercussions and makes the easy call to "go along" when circumstances demand a tough-call approach.

I have encountered nearly every possible combination of good intentions/bad calls, so I can offer the following observation: There's nothing new under the sun, and every company that calls me is experiencing problems because of decisions related to one of 10 things—ideas they should have resisted. Iconic comedian Gilda Ratner used to say, "If it's not one thing, it's another. It's always something." With apologies to Ms. Ratner, I think it's always one of 10 things that we need to repel or do differently.

Linda's Ten Things

1. Senior leaders don't serve as avatars for the behavior they desire in others.

   The word "avatar" has evolved through the ages from the description of Hindu gods that descended from heaven to live among us to a more modern-day definition that includes computer representations of our alter egos or contrived characters. In either sense, the definition describes that which can go beyond human constraints—those earthly bonds that limit our talent and excellence. Effective leaders don't represent deities in human form, but they should set a gold standard that suggests we have the capacity to excel well beyond the shackles we have placed on ourselves.

   When senior leaders fail to serve as avatars for their organizations, two things happen—both bad. First, once-motivated people start to question why they should produce, follow rules, and observe the rules of civility. Second, in tennis parlance, the competition starts to "force" errors, and people begin to make unforced errors too. A forced error occurs when one player hits a good shot, jeopardizing the opponent's ability to react. In these situations, the receiver may have to hustle to the ball, get caught off-balance, or set up a return stroke incorrectly. An unforced error happens when players lose a point by making a mistake in a situation where they should be in full control, like hitting the ball on the wrong part of the racket or hitting the ball too early. Leaders who serve as avatars of excellence force the errors instead of responding to forced errors, and they create an atmosphere that expects and rewards the ability to avoid unforced errors.

2. Both senior leaders and employees confuse strategy and tactics.

   During a recent keynote to an audience of 240, I asked, "Who can recite your mission statement without consulting a mouse pad or the foyer in your building?" About 30 people raised their hands. I then asked them to recite what's on a Big Mac: "Two all-beef patties, special sauce, lettuce, cheese, pickles, onions, on a sesame seed bun." More than half the audience joined me in the recitation. In other words, recalling a commercial that hasn't been on television for more than 20 years, four times as many people in this group could tell me what's on a Big Mac than could tell me their company's mission statement—and these were the senior leaders of those companies!

To quote a popular country/western song, "If you don't stand for something, you'll fall for anything." To build a powerhouse, people need and want to stand for something important—a clear direction everyone understands. But in most organizations, you'll find more people who understand how to run fast than people who can decide which race they should enter . . . more people with well-honed skills for producing results in the short run than visionary strategists.

Certainly, you need both to become a powerhouse, but most organizations are replete with those who can plug ahead and lacking on those who can *plan* ahead; the competition, however, is more likely to outmaneuver you strategically than to outperform you tactically. Your tactical "to-do list" (plugging away) often will keep you in the game today, but only a clear strategy can ensure you'll avoid the also-ran designation. Therefore, as the leader, you must understand the nature of strategy, embrace the changes it brings, set priorities for achieving what your competition can't match, and choose the right people to drive your vision. Only then will you outwit your rivals and claim your unique position of powerhouse.

3. Leaders don't clarify expectations, so they build in too little accountability and too much bureaucracy.

Sending and receiving clear, concrete messages will take you further than any other change can in keeping employees engaged. Most people show up at work WANTING to do a good job. Few people set out to ruin your day. But if they don't understand what you want . . . if you send incongruent verbal and nonverbal messages . . . if you communicate that they can never make you happy, they will give up, and orneriness will set in. Similarly, when leaders create bureaucracy, work bogs down, and results suffer. Or worse, the end starts to justify the means right up until the end isn't the desired future state.

Some sociologists such as Max Weber have argued that bureaucracy constitutes the most efficient and rational way to organize human activity. According to Weber and those of his ilk, systematic processes and organized hierarchies are necessary to maintain order, maximize efficiency, and eliminate favoritism. Most modern organizational theorists don't agree, pointing out that bureaucracies foster complex, inefficient, and inflexible organizations.

Centuries before Weber, a 14th-century English Franciscan friar and scholastic philosopher William of Occam started influencing modern organizational theory—but not enough. Brother Occam suggested that entities must not be multiplied beyond necessity, although these exact words never actually appear in his writing. However, modern organizational practitioners have quickly forgotten or disregarded the sage counsel of the wise brother. He did not actually invent the Occam's Razor—the shaving away of all that is unnecessary—but we base the concept on his teachings. This principle suggests parsimony, economy, and succinctness in problem-solving. It states that the fewest assumptions should be selected—the fewer the better—even though more complicated conclusions might also prove correct.

Today Occam's ideas face mockery every day in most organizations. We have let ourselves become mired in irrelevant but often interesting details because we fear that keeping things simple makes us unsophisticated and uninteresting—which might lead to our unemployment.

For each accepted explanation of a phenomenon, an infinite number of possible and more complex alternatives exist. But these alternatives cost more in time and resources. The HR department that spends four months devising a review process can't spend time on critical issues like recruiting and hiring top talent. The "red tape" of decision making can serve as a formidable archenemy to a powerhouse, but bureaucracy flourishes when people want to build complexity from the building blocks of fear.

Nothing causes people to disengage faster than frustration, especially when leaders hold on to too much and don't delegate enough decision making. If people don't know what decisions they should make independently and which they should make with others, two things happen: Decisions stall, and conflicts occur. When everyone understands the boundaries, job satisfaction soars.

In general, delegate decision-making responsibility and privilege to the lowest level in the organization—along with the authority to carry out decisions and the positive and negative consequences of them. When this happens, bureaucracy disappears.

4. A plan to attract and hire top talent does not exist.

I always tell clients that their second worst nightmare is an idiot with initiative, which begs the question "What's your first worst nightmare?" A smart narcissist.

You don't want either nightmare, because they will cause your "A" players to disengage. Instead, you want a dream come true and the realization that you can't build a powerhouse with average performers in key roles.

The movie *Money Ball*, a 2011 sports drama based on Michael Lewis's book by the same name, should be required viewing for every HR professional. It is the story of the Oakland Athletics' 2002 season and their general manager Billy Beane's attempts to assemble a competitive team. In the film, Beane and assistant GM Peter Brand, faced with the franchise's limited budget for players, build a team of undervalued talent by taking a sophisticated, systematic approach toward scouting and analyzing players. After implementing the new approach, they won 20 consecutive games, an American League record.

5. No systematic approach for wedding career development and succession planning exists.

Most companies do not excel at either, but even those companies that have one or the other don't have a plan for uniting the individual's growth plan to the overall succession plan of the organization. Of course, a true succession plan does tie the two together, but more often than not, organizations develop a replacement plan that doesn't take into account how individuals can prepare for advancement.

A sophisticated and systematic approach to recruitment is a start, but it's only a start. Once you have the major-league players in your doors, you need a plan to keep them there—a plan that will encourage them not to take other recruiters' calls to look for greener pastures, or stadiums to keep the metaphor consistent.

It should all start in the pre-employment interviews. If you can explain to high potential candidates what will be in store for them, you sweeten the deal and make them more likely to sign on. Then you have to deliver on the promise. Turnover among star performers and those in key positions occurs when companies fail to develop a systematic, fair, legal methodology for promotion.

6. Leaders seek team building when they should strive to eliminate turf battles.

At some point the term "team player" started to infect the vernacular of organizations. No one knew what it meant, but everyone agreed that not being one was bad. When people decided to behave badly, to religiously guard their silos, or to generally annoy people, we started to label them "not a team player." We seldom used the term to describe highly motivated, productive performers, just their opposites.

Through this evolution, clients started asking me to help them with teambuilding. When I asked what they wanted to change, more often than not, they wanted more cohesive efforts and committees, not true teambuilding. In one case, however, I received a different response.

The CEO of a publicly traded company specializing in asset management said he wanted more teamwork. I asked how much of his business truly relied on collaboration and how much depended on strong solo performance. He said about 10 percent of the time he needed true cohesion, but that 10 percent accounted for millions of dollars of lost profit. But what he needed more than teamwork was the elimination of turf battles. Once people realized exactly how they needed to behave differently to reach the strategic goals of the firm, they ended the wars and pulled in the same direction. The increase in profits went beyond the few millions we initially addressed to position the company to realize its long-term objective of increasing assets in the next five years.

7. They hold too many meetings that last too long, involve too many people, and focus on information sharing, not decision making.

That's right. Half as many meetings that last half as long for half as many people. When people know you will use their time wisely, they stay engaged. When they know from experience that you will waste it, they disengage immediately.

8. Customers perceive the company's value (products, services, relationships) differently from how employees and leaders do.

We know that most mergers and acquisitions fail or at least fail to deliver on the high hopes of decisions makers. This too often occurs because people have taken their eyes off the customers. It happens in the world of M & A, but companies cleaving to the status quo are guilty too.

Nearly every week, in response to a lengthy explanation about how well he is anticipating customer needs, I ask one of my coaching clients, "What does your buyer want?" He usually says he doesn't know because he hasn't asked. Scheduling calls and meetings with your best customers and asking simply "What else can we do for you?" or "What would it take to make you really happy?" provides a simple, free way to make sure you continue to give your best customers what they think they need and to anticipate what they will likely need in the future.

9. The reward and feedback systems don't encourage productivity and innovation.

When clients tell me they want more teamwork, I ask how they compensate. Nearly always I receive the same answer, "We pay a base salary and bonus that we calculate based on the overall performance of the company." Why, then, would people feel motivated to abandon their proven approach to solo contributing that pays them handsomely for the risky prospect of some other compensation plan? If you want teamwork, reward it.

10. Well-intended people interfere with effectiveness.

Functions in the organization that were created to support the business actually obstruct it. Finance, HR, legal, and IT too often create forms, establish protocols, schedule training, and call meetings that don't actually move the needle on productivity. Instead, these activities distract people from doing their jobs and take time—the most valuable and nonrenewable resource people have.

In virtually every industry, productivity ebbs and flows, depending on myriad factors. When we see these fluctuations, we rightly conclude they have occurred because of an increase or decrease in employee engagement. We also hear countless suggestions for getting this right—for correcting the ebbs and banking on the flows. Now it's time to challenge the ordinary and discover the top things leaders can do to ensure continued and constant engagement while warding off the wrong things—the outdated processes, the wrong processes, and most importantly, the wrong mindset. Make life and work easier for people; let them own their jobs and decisions; and allow them to control their destinies in the company.

Conclusion

I work with organizations whose leaders want to think strategically, grow dramatically, and promote intelligently so they can compete successfully today and tomorrow. This differentiates me from consultants who consider themselves management-repair people—consultants whom junior-level people call for service, much as they would a plumber when a system backs up. Plumbers and management-repair people don't add value; they restore a company to its original condition, correcting the problem but not creating anything better. Too many leaders do the same thing. Why? Mindset.

Bentley Motors has the right mindset—a powerhouse mindset. That company doesn't build a mode of transportation; it is dedicated to developing and crafting the world's most desirable high-performance cars. Decision makers at Bentley Motors understand that people will pay more for the most desirable high-performance cars than they will for a car that merely avoids breaking down on the way to work.

What can you do? Take prudent risks and proactively identify opportunities, because no company has cut its way to success. Move the focus from reducing cost to increasing profits. Identify and eradicate what I call "the business prevention units" in your organization that slow things down in the name of making them better—but they never do. Above all, re-educate your workforce and let them know there's a new sheriff in town who cares about output, not input—profits, not revenues—results, not actions. Salespeople don't make sales calls; they close business. Receptionists don't just answer the phone; machines can do that. They immediately address customer needs and find the fastest solution. Change the mindset, and you can become the company that would put you out of business.

Bentley Motors doesn't have an elevator "pitch" since they sell value, not transportation. What value does your clan offer that you fail to leverage and articulate?

CHAPTER 4

A Funny Thing Happened on the Way to the Bottom Line

Leaders can't control many things at work. In fact, they probably can't control *most* things, but they can control their own *reactions*—their decisions about how they respond to unfortunate, untimely, and unwelcome events. *Only* then can they help direct reports feel authority over their own reactions to unpleasant and unexpected changes. When hard times rear their ugly heads, leaders must be the heroes, the rescuers who look after others and help them keep from losing their constructive perspective and coping resources.

In his work, *Mysterium Coniunctionis* (The Mysterious, Mystical Union), psychologist Carl Jung explained the path of the hero and offered some insights about how a true hero faces and overcomes adversity:

> In myths the hero is the one who conquers the dragon, not the one who is devoured by it. And yet both have to deal with the same dragon. Also, he is no hero who never met the dragon, or who, if he saw it, declared afterwards that he saw nothing. Equally, only one who has risked the fight with the dragon and is not overcome by it wins the hoard, the "treasure hard to attain." He alone has a genuine claim to self-confidence, for he has faced the dark ground of his self and thereby has gained himself. . . . He has arrived at an inner certainty which makes him capable of self-reliance, and attained what the alchemists called the unio mentalis (the unity of mind).

Heroism does not exist without adversity. Consequently, we admire most those who have fought the fight and won, not the ones who have never faced a dragon. The same dragon will devour some people but will be slain by others. The dragon, or the adversity, remains the same; the person opposing the dragon differs. When we develop the necessary coping and decision-making skills to do battle with adversity, we maximize the opportunities for emerging victorious and can then help *others* fend off the dragons too.

Why can some people bounce back from adversity while others languish? Why can some leaders help those around them find the path through the crisis when others can't? To find the answers, I decided to study heroes—people who had overcome some sort of significant adversity and emerged healthy and hardy. I wanted to draw from their experiences in order to advise today's leaders about ways they can help themselves and help others weather the storms that inevitably affect organizations. To find these answers and to better understand how resilient people handle adversity, in 1995 I moved to Pensacola to study the repatriated Vietnam Prisoners of War (VPOWs) at the Robert E. Mitchell POW Center. I found answers—surprising answers.

Funny People Can Be Tough Too

When the Vietnam Conflict ended in 1973, 566 military prisoners of war returned from captivity in Vietnam. More than 40 years later the medical and psychological tests of approximately 300 of these repatriated prisoners—men imprisoned in the north—show few medical, social, and psychological problems. How can this be when other groups in history who have experienced captivity often have shown extreme aftereffects? The answers are varied and complex, but one thing seems clear. The VPOWs, unbeknownst to their captors, employed a system that worked, a system for human connection based on control and grounded in the effective use of humor.

Psychologists tell us human beings want power and authority over their futures—that is, we want to feel we have a say in how things will go for us. When we perceive that our actions will make an outcome likely, we feel optimistic and secure. When we don't, we feel insecure. We feel like victims. Sometimes people stay in a victim's frame of mind after a loss or disappointment. They doubt their capacity to make their lives unfold according to their own aspirations, so they wait for someone to rescue them or to bless them with good fortune. They start to feel undermined and overwhelmed; and they can become totally immobilized.

But the POWs were not victims; they were, with few exceptions, highly educated, well trained military officers. Their captors certainly *victimized* them, but the POWs never saw themselves as victims. They weren't victims because they took *control* of the few things they could control. Their captors told when them what and if they could eat, when they could shower, sleep, and use the toilet. They had no governance over parts of their lives that people normally take for granted. But they did have control over one thing—their humor perspective.

Their need for control served as a framework for the POWs who created and maintained a system of strong interpersonal relationships and group affiliation that helped them survive, in some cases, more than seven years in captivity and to thrive during the years since repatriation. Humor served as one of the elements of that system. The POWs taught each other how to use humor as a weapon for fighting back—as a tool for building cohesion, but the lessons started before their incarceration because each man had grown up in the aviator culture.

Unlike members of the general population, members of the aviation community deal with the reality of death regularly. People from any given corporation frequently face adversity, but few encounter the ultimate dire consequence. The military aviator does. Consequently, aviators have built coping strategies into their culture, and singing songs about death at Friday night happy hour started during previous wars and quickly became a Vietnam Era tradition. The lyrics indicated a desire to overpower death or to remain undaunted by it. The following offer two examples of these kinds of lyrics:

> Dear Mom, your son is dead. He bought the farm today
>
> He drove his OV 10 Down Ho Chi Minh Highway.
>
> He did a rocket pass, and then he busted his ass.
>
> Or
>
> By the fuchsia waterfall one bright and sunny day,

Beside his broken Phantom Jet, the poor young pilot lay.

His parachute hung from a nearby tree. He was not yet quite dead.

Let's listen to the very last words the poor young pilot said:

"I'm going to a better place where everything is right.

Where whisky flows from telephone poles and poker every night.

Where all you have to do all day is sit around and sing,

And the crew chiefs are all women,

Oh, Death where is thy sting?"

"Buying the farm," of course, happened to the other guy, but mocking death helped to disarm the innate fear of flying an aircraft over enemy territory. Instead of viewing death as a taboo or scary subject, this group chose to scoff at it with gallows humor or perhaps even to glorify it by singing about it.

The steeling of oneself to the possibility of death served as one of the preparation strategies these men employed that later served them during captivity—even though they would not have described things this way initially. Thumbing one's nose at the frightful disarms it.

The POWs belonged to a military aviation culture before their shoot-downs, but they also formed a new and different *system* during their captivity that helped them overcome some of the adversity of the situation—a system for resisting and taking control of what they could control, their reactions. The guards forced them to submit and comply with most of their demands, but because of their system of human connection, their group, they were able to rebel, even when prisoners in other captivity situations had not been able to.

The Vietnamese captors, like captors in previous wars, tried to break the power of the group, but failed significantly in key areas. For example, the VPOWs refused to give into the captors' demands that they refrain from addressing each other by rank. The VPOWs also created humor among themselves, and in so doing, exercised control in another sense.

Humor has its basis in the individual, but it manifests itself in interpersonal relationships. When responding to what helped them make it through, the research respondents described humor from both intrapersonal and interpersonal perspectives. That is, they reported a sense of humor within themselves and the laughter they shared with each other. One participant's observation, "The larger the group, the more lighthearted things were. The smaller the group, the more intense things were," reflected the comments of many.

As one man stated, "Believe it or not, even under the almost worst of conditions over there, under the right circumstances, we could laugh." They would say, "Well, boy, we're going to look back on this and laugh, but it sure does hurt now." Another participant added, "The first five months I didn't have a sense of humor. I was having great difficulty finding anything very funny about the situation, and then I discovered by living with other people that we eventually started being awfully funny."

He went on to clarify the kind of humor he often found valuable. "I lived next to a guy in late '67 who had been beaten very severely." After several days of beatings, the friend reported the guards had threatened him that they would break both arms if he did not answer their questions the next day. When asked what he intended to do, he replied, "I don't know. I suppose I'll tap with my cast tomorrow." (The POWs used a code to tap messages through their walls.)

The participant described this as an "almost morbid sense of humor." Another participant called this a type of "in-house humor."

> Those who have not experienced it could not understand how two men could find a discussion about the honey bucket (waste bucket) so funny. Taking off the lid and commenting that one had diarrhea and one was constipated when they had both eaten the same thing was truly funny, but the humor is lost on outsiders.

A third participant called this "had to be there humor." In explaining what he meant, he cited a specific incident. He had passed a worm of substantial length, so he gave it to the guard, thinking the guard would take it to a doctor and request medical attention to kill the obvious parasites in his system:

> So I handed it to him through the bars in the door on a piece of bamboo stick, and the water girls were on the cell block at the time, and I thought, "Hey, he's going to take it to the doctor," and "I'll get some medicine." So he closes the door and then starts chasing the water girls with it, screaming and laughing, and the water cans tipped over.

He further commented that he too remembered mocking the situation to find humor. He mentioned that one of the VPOWs with whom he was communicating tapped to him that when he gets out and "he fills out his critique sheet," he will tell them, "The exercise is real and it lasted too damn long."

We can best appreciate the value of order and self-control in light of the prisoner uncertainties and required compliances. In other words, taking charge of *anything* allowed a perception of some degree of control. For example, getting the best of the guards not only provided humorous remembrances that they could savor later, but it also gave the men a moment of control in what otherwise was a totally uncontrolled situation.

How does a humor perspective give you more control? First, if you control your reactions, you control distractions. If you can find humor in the annoying customer, problem employee, or egregious corporate practice, you can put the unpleasantness in perspective and use your thoughts more productively.

Second, when others think you're funny, and you make them laugh, they will want to build a relationship with you. They will more easily forgive your mistakes and more readily accept your flaws. I read a quote once that said, "Of all those in my life, I love best those who make me laugh." I think most of us share that point of view.

Third, when we laugh, we get more creative. Laughing releases endorphins that cause our brains to function more effectively and efficiently. How often has one person telling a joke triggered a memory in the listener that either engendered another joke or a witty response? That doesn't happen in isolation. Humor has its greatest effect when shared and served hot and spicy.

Why Are Smart People Funny?

Most communication theorists and researchers consider the appropriate use of humor an aspect of communication competence. Nonetheless, one of the obvious and striking facts about humor is that most people most of the time cannot or will not effectively produce humorous messages. Most people usually function as *receivers* rather than as *sources* of humor. We appreciate humor as a positive force in our lives, so why don't more of us rely more heavily on this coping mechanism? Since personality traits and behavioral repertoires differentiate high and low humor-oriented people, we know not everyone has the communication skills, personality traits, or cognitive abilities to create humor. Researchers have found links between a sense of humor and personality traits such as extroversion, lower anxiety levels, internal locus of control, and independence. They have also found a positive relationship between humor and expressiveness, interaction management, and overall impression management.

These descriptions mirror the portrayals researchers offered in the classic aviator personality analyses of the '60s and '70s. These studies found the aviator to be a dominant individual who relates well socially, seeks new situations, and sets high standards—a person who is responsive to the environment, spontaneous, and free of psychopathology. Such a person would, according to the findings of the humor theorists, be a person who would probably enjoy both the reception of humor and the generation of it.[1] This sort of person would also pass the E^5 *Star Performer* litmus test, and most leaders would consider this individual a high potential.

Therefore, we can infer the reason more people do not effectively produce humorous messages: Not everyone has the predisposition or the communicative proficiency to generate funny thoughts—much less humorous messages. The VPOWs did have these traits, however. The personality traits of this group, coupled with their training and maturity, allowed this group to utilize humor as a coping behavior more than other groups in captivity had been able to do.

I found countless examples of the use of humor in the literature both by and about the POWs and in the stories they told me. My favorite involved an exceptionally clever POW, Gerald Venanzi. Many written accounts exist concerning "The Jerry Venanzi Motorcycle," an idea that had its origin with John Thornton during the Korean War. An interview with one of Venanzi's roommates offered an important side to the story.

The roommate reported that one day Venanzi, enjoying a moment outside his cell, noticed some of the other prisoners, tied up and suffering. Venanzi felt helpless, unable to do anything to help his cohorts, helpless except for his ability to create humor. He began to ride an imaginary motorcycle around the complex. The performance, with the supporting antics, had the desired effect among the men. They laughed in spite of their discomfort.

Venanzi's convincing "shows" caused the captors to question his state of mind, so initially they did nothing to stop him. Whenever the captors allowed him outside, Venanzi rode the motorcycle, complete with the appropriate sound effects. He even staged an occasional spill and limped and whined in reaction to it. The motorcycle riding became a source of laughter for the POWs, but the captors allowed him to continue for a period of time. (Apparently some POWS found him so convincing that *they* began to circulate questions and jokes about his stability. The legend gained strength thanks to its basis in humor.) Also, while in solitary, Venanzi created an imaginary companion, a chimpanzee he named Barney Google. The chimpanzee often accompanied Venanzi to interrogations and served as his voice for insults and criticisms. Frequently Venanzi addressed comments to the imaginary companion and reacted to Barney's retorts. On occasion the guards asked what the chimpanzee had said. One guard even offered the animal tea, an offer that Venanzi declined on behalf of Barney, explaining that he didn't like tea. Venanzi's ability to mock the guards and to draw them into the ruse served as fodder for many humorous stories among the POWs. After a period of time, the Vietnamese commander told Venanzi he would have to abandon the motorcycle, explaining that since the other prisoners did not own motorcycles, allowing him to own one hardly seemed fair. Later, when the captors assigned Venanzi roommates, the commander further ordered that they release the chimpanzee since the dirty animal might offend the new cellmates. Venanzi's ability to inject humor and the subsequent humorous stories the POWs told throughout the prison system allowed him and his fellow prisoners a temporary mental escape from the prison walls. To insure accuracy in my research, I sent a transcript of the story of the imaginary monkey to Colonel Venanzi for his approval. He wrote back that he found the work generally factual, but added one comment: "One point does stand out, and I do hope you can correct it before it goes finally into the history books. Barney is a chimpanzee, not a monkey. In fact, he used to get very upset if he was called a monkey. I do hope this can be corrected (for Barney's sake, of course)." When I read the letter, I too laughed, amazed at Venanzi's ability to continue to create mirth through the decades.

Venanzi's creativity helped him help himself and others, but he offers just one example of the role humor played among the VPOWs. Sometimes a man's ability to think fast saved himself and others from dire consequences. One repatriated POW reported that he doubted how he should answer the captors' questions concerning the swimming pools aboard his former aircraft carrier. Of course, these swimming pools did not exist, but this VPOW inferred that at some point another prisoner must have falsified this information under duress. To blatantly deny the existence of these pools risked torture for himself or of the other prisoner. Instead, he thought of a reasonable explanation for the misunderstanding. He assured the quizzer that the other prisoner must have been referring the whirlpools that were in the sick bay. The captors had no knowledge of whirlpools, so the prisoner's explanation seemed a rational explanation for the confusion, and it generated a story that would provide hours of entertainment for the other POWs.

Another VPOW, who had been forced to give classified information concerning the maximum airspeed of his airplane, gave an inaccurately low speed that the captors questioned. They pressured him to tell the truth, stating that another prisoner had given a higher airspeed for the same aircraft. Thinking fast, the POW replied, "Well, that guy is a major. I'm only a lieutenant. They don't let lieutenants fly as fast as they let the majors fly." The explanation seemed reasonable to the captors; it allowed the lieutenant to avoid further coercion while not giving classified information; and it served as a source of laughter for the POWs for many years.

Anytime the prisoners tricked the captors, they gained a sense of control and used the ruse to generate stories throughout the POW communication system. These stories served many functions, one of the most important ones being that they allowed the POWs to enjoy the benefits of humor and to realize they had control over their reactions, even though they had control over little else.

Kiss Humor Right on the Lips

References to the use of humor occur in much of the captivity-related literature. Even in the Holocaust literature we find references to the use of humor as a coping strategy. Author, physician, and Holocaust survivor Viktor Frankl recalled, "Humor was another of the soul's weapons in the fight for self-preservation."[2] Realizing this, Frankl suggested to a friend that they promise each other to invent at least one amusing story daily about some incident that could happen one day after their liberation. Frankl found these stories allowed the prisoners to escape the confines of the wall, if just for a few seconds.

For example, Frankl told the friend, a surgeon, they would be unable to lose the habits of camp life when they returned to their former work. Since they had become accustomed to responding to the foreman's command for "Action! Action!" they would not be able to function without this encouragement. Once back in the operating room, Frankl assured the surgeon, he would be performing a big abdominal operation. Suddenly an orderly would rush in announcing the arrival of the senior surgeon by shouting, "Action! Action!" Other prisoners joked that forgetting themselves at future dinner engagements, they might beg the hostess to ladle the soup "from the bottom," a request made by prisoners hoping to scoop the treasured vegetables instead of the watery soup on the top.

The prisoners also extended this type of making light of the intolerable to the jokes about the Capos, the prominent prisoners who received special privileges, often in payment for mistreating fellow prisoners. In referring to a particularly troublesome Capo, one prisoner mocked, "Imagine! I knew that man when he was only the president of a large bank. Isn't it fortunate that he has risen so far in the world?"[3]

With the overwhelming amount of Holocaust literature addressing the depression and apathy that existed among the prisoners, the researcher begins to realize the value of a kind of thumbing one's nose at an unspeakable or frightening situation. There is no conclusive evidence that this type of deriding played a critical role in the hardiness of the concentration camp prisoners, but since several researchers mention this type of behavior and expound on the importance of it, the idea seems credible.

Ford and Spaulding mentioned the importance of humor in reference to the captivity of the Pueblo crew, calling humor an "ego mechanism." In fact, these researchers found it to be even more helpful to the prisoners than religion. They pointed out, "Humor was an ability to joke about the characteristics of their captors and to give the guards (and each other) nicknames."[4]

Nearly every book written by or about the VPOWs mentioned some humorous story or incident. Repatriated prisoner of war (RPOW) Porter Halyburton (1989) pointed out, "Humor is often an important element of survival in difficult circumstances, and it was in ours. We used to say, 'You have to get here early to get the good deals.'"[5]

This sort of mocking, or ridiculing humor sustained many of the men during captivity. In this same vein, RPOW Ralph Gaither wrote, "Humor in the bleakest of circumstances is a characteristic of Americans. That wisecracking and laughter in the face of torture and inhumanity announced to our captors that any capitulation to them would be only fleeting and insincere."[6]

Gaither described jeering and finding humor as a covert fighting-back posture, a way of taking control of one's reaction when he could not have control of the situation.

Like captives from other wars, the VPOWs experienced little governance over their lives. The loss of power in prison felt so pervasive and profound the POWs had to find control in whatever ways they could. Humor provided one of those ways. Without the use of humor, a formidable weapon for coping with loss of control in other aspects of life, the prisoners would have experienced almost total loss of mastery in their lives. Grasping what little power they had helped them clutch the reins momentarily and avoid the feelings of capitulation to which Gaither referred.

Many similarities exist among groups who have used humor to cope with imprisonment, but some significant differences exist as well. The comparison of VPOW literature with that of other groups who have been in captivity shows stark differences that might help explain why the Vietnam group has remained resilient since repatriation. Unlike any other group that has experienced long-term captivity, the VPOWs who were imprisoned in Hanoi were usually college educated, chronologically mature, healthy, trained aviators. Also the majority of the prisoners had received some form of POW and survival training. Those who had not received formal training received advice and direction from those who had. No other group of World War II, concentration camp, Korea, or Pueblo prisoners met these criteria. In short, this Vietnam POW group was better prepared than any other in recent history to withstand the rigors of captivity. However, they had another important difference: Most of these prisoners possess a somewhat typical "aviator personality," which includes a relatively advanced ability to use humor, a component of communication competence.

What lessons do the POW stories imply for business leaders? First, leaders can focus on their own humor perspective. That starts with reframing. Humor researchers agree that adversity plus time equals humor. Why wait? The story about our most embarrassing moment, car problems, home repairs, and even health scares can seem funny when we look in the rearview mirror. When you're tempted to think, "Someday I'll laugh about this," why not make that day today? The personal stories, written accounts, and lore imply that it's a good idea to embrace humor in times of adversity. But in dire circumstances, you'll need to kiss humor right on the lips.

We Trust People Who Make Us Laugh, Why?

Ralph Waldo Emerson once said, "If you want to rule the world, you must keep it amused," and Victor Borge added, "Laughter is the shortest distance between two people." Intrapersonal communication, or communication within self, is of particular interest to any study of the VPOWs because, unlike prisoners in most other captivity situations, the Vietnam group experienced long periods of isolation. Virtually all VPOWs spent at least a few days in solitary confinement, and some spent several years alone. They had almost no opportunity for face-to-face communication with other Americans and limited chances to communicate through walls or by note. Consequently, each man was left to devise his own method for coping with his situation.

For most of the VPOWs, coping with captivity involved developing mirth and honing humor skills. One research participant remembered his first true realization of the value of humor in December of 1966, about ten months after his capture—a day he described as a turning point for him. He had been in solitary confinement and was peeking through a hole in the wall, watching the guards. One guard asked another a question, so the first guard handed him his rifle; then he took off his bullet belt; then he took off his huge coat and reached in his pocket. He struggled to get something out of his pocket and pulled out an enormous clock. The first guard had obviously asked what time it was, and the second guard had to undress to tell him.

> He didn't have a watch; he had a "Baby Ben" clock stuck in his pants pocket. I'd been beaten pretty severely every day for most of a month, and I was just absolutely rolling on the floor. When this was all over, I realized, "I thought I was going to die today; and all I did today was have a good laugh."

That was the day it became apparent to him that humor would play a major role in his survival.

On that December day, this POW learned to trust his own humor perspective. He realized he had the capacity to make himself laugh. Eventually, he came to rely on his capacity to find humor in dire circumstances and built trust that he'd be able to continue to do so. Similarly, in modern business settings, we like and trust people who serve as sources of humor because they quite simply make us feel better.

For instance, in 2016 I found myself in South Florida directly in the path of Hurricane Matthew. The Four Seasons Hotel received a mandatory evacuation order for all of us staying at their resort in West Palm Beach. The well-trained staff helped us change our airline reservations and find rooms at the Airport Hilton so we'd be in position for early-morning flights. Everyone reacted professionally and helped us devise a plan to safety. I will always remember the exemplary service of the Four Seasons staff, but I will remember with affection the Southwest Airlines captain who spoke to us right before takeoff.

As we settled into the very crowded plane with no assigned seats and watched the winds pick up on the runway, the captain informed us he had a hurricane update: "I want to give you an update on the hurricane. It is now reported that it won't hit Florida. Instead, it's headed right to Baltimore," our destination. The passengers burst into laughter and applause, grateful for the release of tension and fear.

Southwest Airlines is legendary for encouraging its crew members to use humor in their announcements, something that helps to reduce nervousness in the anxious traveler. They have built a reputation for making people feel better, and other leaders can too. Sometimes you'll find it is as simple as giving people permission to laugh at themselves and the absurdity of life.

Be More Funny; Make More Money

Understanding the benefits of using humor appropriately is the first step, actualizing this knowledge the second. Help your organization become a place where the best people can do their best work—and have fun while they're doing it. How does humor help with tough calls? Here's how:

- Humor can diffuse a bad situation.
  I seem to get stuck in Chicago airports quite often because most of my flights connect through there, and I have clients there. In the summer, you can count on thunderstorms wreaking havoc. In the winter, snow and ice jump on the flight-delay bandwagon. At O'Hare, you'll find American and United gate agents attempting to placate disgruntled passengers, usually with little success. Voice volume increases; veins stick out; and tempers flare. At Midway, on the other hand, you'll find Southwest agents using humor to reduce tension. How do they do it? Southwest makes hiring funny people a priority. In fact, in their pre-employment interviews, they ask applicants to describe a situation in which they used humor on the job, a question that gives interviewers a sense of

whether the person would fit in at Southwest. This helps them hire those who will support their culture of mirth.
- Laughter can reduce the experience of pain and raise a person's pain threshold.

In 1964, doctors diagnosed Norman Cousins with Ankylosing Spondylitis, a rare disease of the connective tissue, and told him he had only months to live and only a 1 in 500 chance of survival. He didn't accept the diagnosis. Instead, he sought unconventional means for halting the disease and for controlling the pain associated with it. He purchased a movie projector and funny movies, including the Marx Brothers and the Candid Camera shows. According to Cousins, laughing allowed him several pain-free hours, and extended his life 26 years!

Can we prove laughter extended Cousins's life? No. My fellow humor researchers have tried to prove that laughter affects the immune system, the body's ability to resist pain, and various other aspects of physical health; however, the evidence remains largely anecdotal. Inflicting pain in a laboratory situation reeks of unethical practices, but some researchers have made attempts. For example, researchers asked students to submerge their arms in ice water and keep it there as long as they could. The findings suggest that those who watched humor videos could withstand the discomfort of the ice water longer than the control group. But anyone who has experienced child birth knows that a cold arm and true pain exist in two separate worlds. Cousins did leave us the legacy of his personal research and chronicled it in a collection of best-selling books on healing, including his 1980 autobiographical memoir, *Human Options: An Autobiographical Notebook*.
- Humor unites.

There are topics that can be universally humorous: misers, bad drivers, absent-minded people, kids, pets, indignities, and embarrassments. Each workplace has its unique sources of humor too. When leaders give people permission to enjoy funny or ridiculous stories and to engage in self-effacing humor, they open the possibilities of making work more fun. Most of us spend more hours with our colleagues than we do with our family members. Doesn't it make sense for us to discover new ways of building rapport and endearing ourselves to one another? When we feel connected to others through humor, we feel inclusion, affection, and a sense of control. That equips us to handle change more gracefully too.

- Humor helps us avoid running out of altitude, airspeed, and ideas at the same time.

Since the dawn of aviation, pilots have cautioned each other not to run out of altitude, airspeed, and ideas at the same time—good idea for those who fly the vastness of the skies and applicable to business leaders too. In a metaphorical sense, "altitude" is the ability to keep things in perspective.

When we think of airspeed, we think of velocity, forces that make us go forward. Research tells us relationships serve as one of the main sources of fuel that helps us accelerate, with communication a primary tool for developing closeness. However, the VPOWs found communication was difficult, dangerous, and sometimes nearly impossible. Yet, it became a priority.

In 1965, Bob Shumaker, an early prisoner, realized the POWs were going to need a communication system. For more than four months, Shumaker endured solitary confinement, but he knew the Vietnamese had captured another American: Hayden Lockhart. Through the cracks in his walls, Shumaker observed another American taking his waste bucket to the communal facility. He knew he needed to make contact. After much deliberation, Shumaker decided he would write a three-word note on toilet paper and hide it behind a piece of cement in the latrine. But he had to be very careful about what he wrote—it couldn't be very much, and it had to be exact. Above all else, whatever he wrote, it could put neither Shumaker nor Lockhart at risk of torture if the captors discovered they had tried to communicate. Shumaker wrote three words: "Scratch your balls."

His thinking was twofold. He wanted to write something that an American would know only another American would write so that the person receiving the note would not suspect a trick. Second, he wanted to devise a signal that the captors would not find suspicious.

He wrote the note, and day after day, he stood peeking through the cracks in the mortar in his room, and day after day, Lockhart came out of the latrine and made no gesture. Finally, one day, Lockhart came out and made a huge display of scratching the region in question and facing every part of the compound—ensuring that the person who wrote the note would realize that he had received it. Admiral Shumaker told me in 1995 the most complicated communication system in history was born with a scratch of a crotch.

The POWs knew they would need other ways of communicating, even if they risked torture in the future as they had initially. Not too long after the day Lockhart started the communication system, the captors assigned Shumaker some roommates, including Smitty Harris who remembered the "tap code" from survival school. The Tap Code, which I mentioned previously, became the most sophisticated communication system in POW history. Originally, former POWs had devised this code to serve as a communication system for getting policy throughout the POW camp, but it quickly became a way for sharing jokes, staying connected, and building morale.

We know humor helps us avoid mental rigidity—to "play" with ideas that help us devise more creative solutions than we would otherwise discover. No one told the POWs their humor would help them create the ideas that would help them cope. Instead, they stumbled onto the realization that humor and three other things would help them survive: a belief in God, feelings of connection to other POWs, and a commitment to something-bigger-than-I-am orientation.

- Humor can make others want to pack your parachute. Charles Plumb, a U.S. Navy fighter pilot, was shot down May 19, 1967 and spent six years in the Hanoi Hilton. One day after his repatriation, he and his wife were sitting in a restaurant when a man at a nearby table approached him and said, "You're Captain Plumb! You flew jet fighters in Vietnam from the aircraft carrier *Kitty Hawk*. You were shot down!"

When Plumb asked, "How in the world did you know that?" the man replied, "I packed your parachute. Guess it worked!" Plumb replied, "It sure did. If your chute hadn't worked, I wouldn't be here today." Plumb realized that he didn't remember this sailor, but he quite literally owed his life to him.[7]

Leaders often don't recognize those in the organization who pack their parachutes, but they too rely on these loyal employees for support of all kinds. When we can share a laugh, or even a mirthful moment with someone upon whom we rely, we communicate our appreciation and commitment to building rapport. Humor helps.

Conclusion

To prevent a disjunction of the self and to find meaning in a situation void of meaning, the VPOWs relied on resources many of them did not know they had. Their internal sense of mirth and humor, their reliance on one another, and their group interactions all combined to create a system for survival. Their humor perspective provided the framework for discovering how to cope with their captivity, and their commitment to one another gives an important perspective about what contributes to coping. The role humor can play in bouncing back from adversity, especially when we are linked to others who will help us laugh, seems critical.

Throughout history each prisoner of war was an individual who had to develop his own system of coping with captivity. His uniqueness required him to look inside himself and to marshal resources perhaps even he did not know he possessed. The situation challenged him to find some sense in a senseless situation. Humor provides one way of doing that.

Humor provided a way for the POWs to take a modicum of control and to remain connected to others. The VPOWs' lessons about using humor to restore one's perspective and to build rapport and connection with others are poignant. They bolstered the prisoners' humor in a strong social structure that served as a powerful civilizing force that discouraged any antisocial slip into a jungle mentality. Certainly, human reactions are complicated, and an individual's uniqueness must be balanced against our species' commonality, but the VPOWs offer too many examples of people thriving for us to ignore their numbers and coping skills. A historical comparison of groups who have experienced captivity, trauma, and atrocities, and an analysis of their ability to cope by using humor allow the average person to infer that the use of humor might also be beneficial during times of less extreme stress.

The VPOW accounts indicate these men formed a system that defined and encouraged humor among the group's members. These men relied on humor not in spite of the crisis but *because* of it. Control is central to individuals' health, their personal benefits, and, in the case of the Vietnam POWs, their actual survival.

CHAPTER 5

Brainwashing or Persuasion?

Against a backdrop of GM's recall scandal and Volkswagen's 2014 emissions scandal, painting modern executives as villains and blaming corporations for all manner of societal ills has nearly become a national pastime. While we still admit that big businesses provide jobs, develop technological advancements, and provide needed products and services, we have sunk into an anticorporate movement. We accuse corporations of general malfeasance while specifically blaming leaders for undermining the dignity of employees, corrupting cultures, and compromising societal mores.

When and how did things change? Hollywood producers of shows like *Mad Men* don't hesitate to paint the executives of the '50s and '60s as loud, vein-popping, spittle-generating producers and purveyors of both fear and salty language. Even though they didn't engage in the Patton-esque behavior of slapping slaking subordinates, back then, some leaders nonetheless terrorized those in their organizations—using dominance and force to achieve the results they wanted. The Human Resource movement may have originated in the 1920s, but behavior in organizations didn't *really* start to improve until much later, as the result of social-reform efforts, new legislation, and evolving social norms. Today, with the accusations of inflated CEO pay, pay-for-performance board expectations, increased governmental oversight, the accusations of malfeasance seem to have come full circle.

Do modern corporations practice mind control when they attempt to create a workforce that shares a common culture? Could critics have it right? Does corporate brainwashing exist as an insidious attempt to create a worldwide monocultural network of producers, consumers, and managers? Or, might there be another explanation—a rational, nonjudgmental way of thinking about the decisions leaders should make to influence those in their chains of command?

The Leader's Obligation to Influence

Not all great influencers are leaders, but all great leaders are influencers. We look to these great leaders for advice and direction. We give them power and trust their judgment because they add value to our lives—or we hope they will. They use their expertise, wisdom, and authority to *guide*, not force, solutions. Arguably, sometimes we don't *choose* those who have power over us. Often a board of directors or others senior to us in an organization make the pivotal decisions about who will lead us. But ultimately, *we* decide whom we will follow—whom we will allow to influence and persuade us.

Influence involves the ability to sway opinions, attitudes, behavior, and taste. Influence doesn't necessarily involve pressure or dominance, but it does involve the capacity to demand that others pay heed. Influence involves inducing others to change their behaviors without the exertion of control or the authority that comes with positional power. Persuasion goes a step further. It involves an active attempt to convince others to change—to modify their beliefs or behaviors.

What role does your executive presence—the manner and attitude that draw people to you—play in swaying outcomes? The leader–follower phenomenon illustrates one of the most intriguing expressions of human behavior. Since the beginning of civilization, people have sought answers to the questions of who becomes a leader and why. Philosophers, political scientists, and psychologists have produced extensive literature on leaders and leadership, but despite this, they haven't reached consensus as to why and under what circumstances some become leaders and others remain followers—why we allow certain people to influence and persuade us while we ignore the attempts of others. We still don't agree on a universal theory of leadership either, and no one has a precise formula for producing leaders. Answers remain elusive. Furthermore, the debate continues about whether effective leadership and successful management are synonymous.

Yet, research and investment in leadership have grown exponentially in the past century. We may not have it right, but we haven't given up on it either. We have moved from the trait, style, and situational leadership theories and now focus on what an individual leader *does* to a passive recipient—the follower—and on what happens when people work together to change things.

The 1980s and '90s brought us transformational leadership theories that recognized the dynamic nature of the relationships between leader and follower, but a disconnect between theory and practice persists. Despite calls for more inclusion and democracy in decision making and a shift from *who* makes decisions to *how* leadership affects outcomes, the tough calls remain squarely on the shoulders of those at the top. And while dominance and force have lost their allure, leaders must still persuade to influence. In short, they must balance firmness and fairness to sway outcomes ethically but effectively.

How does a leader's track record for effective decisions encourage followers to support future decisions? In *The Magnetic Boss* I introduced the F^2 Leadership Model which explains the *behaviors*—no the skills, talents, attitudes, or preferences—executives need to display to be effective. An F^2 leader balances concern for task accomplishment and people issues. More follower-driven than leader-driven, the model keeps the leader's focus on those who count—the people in the organization who will define success.

The model explores two key dimensions of leadership: relationship behaviors, like fairness, and task behaviors, like firmness. When leaders compromise the balance between fairness and firmness, they lose their effectiveness and jeopardize that of their direct reports. The model helps them analyze what they do and then make choices to move toward F^2 behavior.

firm

Aggressor
- Overly task focused
- Controlling
- Domineering
- Insensitive

F2 leader
- Firm but fair
- Assertive
- Responsive
- Results oriented

Quit 'n' stay
- Apathetic
- Not task oriented
- Not people focused
- Passive/aggressive

Accommodater
- Harmony seeking
- Too friendly
- Eager to please
- Not task oriented

fair

Fairness costs little but pays handsomely. Why, then, don't more leaders manage to behave fairly? In a nutshell, fairness and responsiveness take time—the nonrenewable commodity that so many executives hold most dear. Jumping in to fix problems, telling people what to do instead of mentoring them, and maintaining an action orientation requires less time than balancing your concern for people with your concern for task accomplishment.

Fairness doesn't demand popular decisions, which don't usually define great, much less adequate, leadership. Fairness positions the leader to make *tough* calls—which usually means unpopular calls—calls that those in the chain of command must accept and execute. We know that pain pushes until passion pulls. Great leaders recognize they have to play a role in creating the passion.

When I work with executives, most often I find leaders who know what should happen—what needs to happen—but they don't want to make the decision to *make it happen*. Why? Usually these executives know the best course of action, but because that path requires upsetting people, making unpopular choices, or terminating someone, they put off, rather than address, the problem. To help move them to action, to balance firmness and fairness, I urge them to ask themselves these questions:

- How much longer can this go on before I experience more negative consequences?
  Doing nothing can be a pricey proposition. Still, leaders often fail to see this. Instead, they stick with the status quo, erring on the side of fairness, or at least their *perception* of fairness. Long-range fairness, however, usually requires short-term firmness.
- What else would this person have to do before I'd fire him or her?
  A wrong-minded attempt to remain "fair" can keep a leader from terminating an employee who has not responded to feedback. Fairness demands the boss give feedback, coach the person to improve performance, and set clear expectations, but it does not and should not require the boss to accommodate unproductive behavior.

- What opportunities might I miss if I do nothing?
  Most leaders understand the concept of opportunity cost or opportunity interest. Both involve the lost opportunities we experience when we don't choose the best way to spend or invest money. Similarly, we have opportunity costs when we don't have the best people, focused strategy, or implementation plan in place. Leaders see or perceive actual costs, however, more readily than they notice opportunity costs. They will keep underperformers in place too long, failing to see what *could* happen if stars were to take their places.

People want control of their own lives, so by extension, they want leaders who inspire confidence that they have the wherewithal to influence desirable outcomes—the ability to create the perception that someone capable has control, even when we don't feel we do. One of the strangest things about the perception of control is that it confers many of the psychological benefits of genuine control. About the only group of people who seem generally immune to this illusion are the clinically depressed. Studies about them have led some researchers to conclude that the feeling of control—whether real or illusory—constitutes one of the wellsprings of mental health. Why, then, do we seek those who make us feel secure, those people who help us believe we are in charge? It feels good—period. As Daniel Gilbert, author of *Stumbling on Happiness*, pointed out, "The act of steering one's boat down the river of time is a source of pleasure, regardless of one's port of call."[1]

Research also tells us humans are the only creatures that know how to think about the future. In fact, some studies suggest we think about the future about one hour out of every eight. For some, this time travel into the future creates anxiety. We worry about what we can't control, may not know to control, or won't have the resources to control. For other healthier people, taking a trip into the future ignites anticipation, excitement, and joy. Our brains insist on projecting us into the future, so we welcome those people into our lives who can help us paint credible pictures of what it might look like. Leaders with advanced analytical reasoning abilities see the future as open and malleable, and they perceive an obligation to take us there, if only in our current thinking.

Animals must *experience* an event in order to learn about its pleasures and pains, but our powers of foresight allow us to imagine that which has not yet happened and hence spare ourselves the hard lessons of experience. We want—and we *should* want—to control the direction of our boats because some futures are better than others, and even from this distance we should be able to tell which are which.[2]

But we can't. Often, the future fundamentally differs from how it appears through our crystal balls. We learn from past disappointments that we frequently suffer from illusions of foresight. Therefore, we trust—or at least we *want* to trust—the leaders who share the journey with us. We tacitly give them permission to persuade us and hope they won't abuse the privilege of persuasion.

Leaders don't have the responsibility for making people happy, but they can systematically avoid making people unhappy. They don't have to possess a crystal ball—but it helps. Or, at least they need to know how to anticipate the consequences of their tough calls. The leader doesn't need to be the smartest person in the room, but she or he should have hired that person. Influence remains the one thing leaders can't delegate entirely, which carries two obligations: The responsibility to influence those in the organization and those outside it. Culture emanates from the top, so the leader's tough calls influence everything. Knowing this, what can a leader do to inspire, stimulate, and reassure without crossing an ethical line and venturing into the realm of coercion?

What Is Brainwashing?

Espoused beliefs reflect those perceptions that an organization's leaders consider "correct." Over time, members of an organization learn that certain beliefs work to reduce uncertainty, so these beliefs gradually develop into an articulated set of norms and operational rules of behavior that serve as a guide for dealing with ambiguity or difficult events. As new members join the organization, others influence them through education about these beliefs.

Brainwashing, on the other hand, involves thought reform—the impairment of autonomy, a disruption of affiliations, and the involuntary reeducation of personal values. Most psychologists believe brainwashing can happen under the right conditions, but they see it as improbable and rare, usually only occurring in a prisoner-of-war situation. In fact, much of what we understand about brainwashing surfaced after the Korean War when psychologists wanted to know how the POW experience had changed military members.

Researchers wanted to understand how the Chinese had swayed many of our soldiers, as evidenced by reports of extensive collaboration with captors, using propaganda broadcasts fellow prisoners made and using letters and other evidence. Researchers concluded the Chinese had attempted to wage an "ideological war" and wondered whether the Chinese had "brainwashed" our troops, what this meant, and what means they had used. Researchers concluded the much-feared Communist program of brainwashing involved an intensive indoctrination program and sophisticated techniques of undermining the social structure of the prisoner group. The Chinese did elicit collaboration but *not* ideological change of any sort. In other words, the Chinese failed in their indoctrination attempts, but they did exercise social control.

Edgar Schein, the prominent researcher on the project, observed:

> If one conceives of brainwashing as a process of producing genuine, extensive, and *lasting* belief, attitude, and value change in a person resisting such change, then only the small number of American civilians imprisoned on the Chinese mainland are true cases of brainwashing.

He further explained why most researchers have abandoned discussions of true brainwashing, preferring the term "coercive persuasion" as a more accurate description of what happened to the Korean POWs.[3]

Drawing from his research, Schein concluded several important lessons for business leaders. For instance, for influence to occur, there must be a motive to change, a direction for the change, and a reward for the change. He added that many variables determined influence or resistance, with "struggle" as the consistent common denominator. Coercive persuasion involved changes in perceptions of, beliefs about, and attitudes toward the self and toward interpersonal relationships. Schein's seminal work, therefore, helped us understand the role others play in the changes we make in our attitudes, beliefs, and behavior. He added an important note that the process of persuasion can have unanticipated and undesirable consequences. He warned that too much ritualization of belief, what we now call "culture," can lead to a gradual atrophy of creative abilities leaders should preserve and harness for accomplishing their goals.[4]

Following the Korean War, journalist and U.S. intelligence agent Edward Hunter offered a definition of brainwashing:

> Brainwashing is an effort to put a man's mind into a fog so that he will mistake what is true for what is untrue, what is right for what is wrong, and come to believe what did not happen actually had happened until he ultimately becomes a robot for the Communist manipulator.

Weapons of Mass Persuasion

Political scientist Bernard Cohen said, "The press may not be successful most of the time in telling people what to think, but it is stunningly successful in telling them what to think about." Like their media counterparts, business leaders can't brainwash, nor should they engage in coercive persuasion, but certainly they can create a laserlike focus on critical issues.

When I witness the failure of a senior leader, a lack of focus on important matters most often explains the crash. They have failed to tell employees what to think about. Too frequently these leaders fail to zero in on the critical few and put aside the trivial many. The trivial many, most often emotional reactions, cloud their vision and create the fog to which Hunter referred—even without the brainwashing. When this happens, people start chasing the rabbits back down the holes, all the while running scared from real or imagined predators.

For example, when I coached Jack, a VP of sales for a large publicly traded company, I noticed his perfectionistic tendencies caused him to lose his focus. He prided himself for having a keen eye for the details, a behavior that had served him well through his career. However, when he advanced to the VP level, his strong detail orientation started to hinder, not help, him. He wanted *everything* to be a priority, so nothing was. He gave the same consideration to things that didn't need his attention as he did to those that demanded it. His emotions began to rule when logic should have reigned. Thanks to a CEO who possessed a laserlike focus on critical issues, Jack put aside the inconsequential distractions and concentrated on important issues.

When leaders arm themselves and those around them with advanced critical-thinking skills, two things happen. First, they attract others who share their advanced skills for discernment. These people look at the organizational landscape and they not only distinguish the forest from the trees, they differentiate the kinds of trees, their characteristics, and their value to the organization. This ability to see distinctions and to communicate them to others equips these leaders to influence.

Leaders often ignore a related weapon for fighting predators: noise reduction. We know environmental, actual noise adversely affects students in schools near train tracks and airports. Psychological or emotional noise affects employees in much the same way. "Noise" exists in every industry, company, political campaign, and social justice movement. Leaders allow and even generate a tendency to lead with tactics instead of objectives, a particularly insidious form of this noise.

For example, The Occupy Wall Street protest began September 17, 2011, in Zuccotti Park, near New York's financial district. In general, the protesters wanted to end social and economic inequality worldwide. Later, more specific goals to redistribute income, demand bank reform, create jobs, and forgive student loans emerged. Dissenters claimed the group's ultimate goal was to end capitalism. Officials demanded the group disband on November 11, just two months after its inception. I don't know of any changes that happened as a result of the movement, and I haven't heard one story of a single person who benefited from the protest.

In addition to lacking a clear vision for the protest, organizers did not establish how they would measure their success. Ultimately, they went home when forced to do so and when the weather turned cold, but not before they alienated business owners near the park whose properties protesters damaged.

Specifically, leaders at Burger King and Panini and Company Café reported altercations with protesters. The owner of Panini, Stacey Tzortzatos, found her tolerance in short supply when someone broke the sink in the restroom. She installed a $200 lock on that door to thwart nonpaying customers—a decision that angered protesters and brought her unwelcome publicity.

Business leaders falter in much the same ways. They determine a method before they define a direction, metrics, or success indicators. In the process, they also alienate would-be supporters or stakeholders who might have supported them had they understood the proposed change. Madness ensues. The "noise" distracts everyone from what must happen, and the focus turns to *how* it will happen.

When an organization faces a significant decision, senior leaders bear the responsibility for framing the problem for themselves and others. The ability to frame a problem serves as a powerful tool for enhancing and facilitating discussion of the problem. Like a frame around a picture, this action can determine how we view a situation and how we interpret it. Often the best frame for a picture enhances the artwork it surrounds without calling attention to itself. It calls attention to the piece of work and sets it off from the other objects in the room.

Similarly, in decision making, a frame creates a mental border that encloses a particular aspect of a situation, to outline its key elements and to create a structure for understanding it. Mental frames help us navigate the complex world, so we can avoid solving the wrong problem or solving the right problem in the wrong way. Our personal frames form the lenses through which we view the world. Education, experience, expectations, and biases shape and define our frames, just as the collective perceptions of a group's members will mold theirs.

When leaders frame a decision, they explain their focus and influence how others should see the situation. They spotlight the relevant part of the discussion and help everyone sidestep or ignore everything inconsequential. In addition to influencing others' perceptions, framing reduces mental clutter, fosters agreement, and accelerates movement. Everything inside the frame matters. Everything outside does not.

Because people often react unconsciously to their frame of reference, leaders can help group members become aware of the frames they bring to the wall. Often these frames represent a stagnant, we've-always-done-it-that-way argument for sticking with the status quo.

Whether a leader offers the initial frame or someone else does, don't automatically accept it. Instead, try to reframe the problem in various ways. Ask, "Is this really the issue?" Force yourself and others to get to the core of the problem without being distracted by symptoms, indications, causes, or effects.

Even the questions themselves can influence outcomes when they test the frame and force new perspectives by encouraging comparisons:

- Are you dissatisfied with _____ or _____?
- How would you compare _____ with what has happened before? How is this different?
- When something like this happened before, what worked?
- What resources will you commit to this?
- To what extent are you willing to change the status quo? Structure? Reward system? Reporting relationships?

These questions frame the issues from different reference points and allow those in a group to discover their frames and the frames of those who disagree with them. People who understand the power of framing also know its capacity to exert influence. They have learned that establishing the framework within which others will view the decision is tantamount to determining the outcome. As a senior leader, you have both the right to and the responsibility for shaping outcomes. Even if you can't eradicate all the distortions and noise ingrained in your thinking and that of others, you can build tests like this into your decision-making processes and improve the quality of your choices. Effective framing offers one way to do that. These criteria can help:

1. Distinguish fact from opinion—evidence from inference.
2. Address areas of agreement before tackling conflicts.
3. Determine causes before exploring options.
4. Paraphrase and restate at each major crossroad.
5. Reduce cognitive dissonance. Ask, "Why am I seeing *that* if you're telling me *this*?"

6. Identify patterns and recurring themes.

Effective framing helps embrace "Occam's Razor," the principle I mentioned in chapter 3. The term "razor" refers to the act of shaving away everything that stands in the way of the simplest explanation, making as few assumptions as possible and eliminating those that make no difference.

Thomas Aquinas recognized the value of simplicity a century earlier when he offered, "If a thing can be done adequately by means of one, it is superfluous to do it by means of several; for we observe that nature does not employ two instruments where one suffices." Albert Einstein added his brilliance to the discussion with his observation: "Theories should be as simple as possible, *but no simpler.*"

In business situations, the simplest explanation that covers all the facts usually offers the best and most compelling solution, but uncovering it may not be quite so easy. People complicate decisions because they can't separate the critical elements from the unimportant elements. They lump together the "must haves" with the "wants" and even throw in some "nice to haves." They introduce ways to execute a decision before making the goal of the decision clear. They muddy the waters by trying to make *all* aspects of the situation a top priority, and skirt around the periphery of the problem instead of cutting to its core. Leaders become more influential when they help their teams shave away all but the simplest representation of the issue, reduce labor intensity, and concentrate on the problem.

One persuasion technique involves highlighting each person's "loss aversion" tendency. Most people most of the time loathe the idea of giving up what they already have or enjoy. Therefore, protecting what we have often motivates us to act, even when we don't necessarily like the action.

For instance, every fall, doctors engage in a loss aversion campaign to influence patients to get their flu shots. No one wants to have another shot, and most people dislike taking the time to get one. However, when we believe the inoculation will prevent a significant loss of our health, or in extreme cases, cause our death, we comply with doctors' orders.

Contrast the success of flu shot crusades with attempts to persuade people to join gyms. Nearly everyone agrees exercise improves health, yet few take the steps to improve the health they already enjoy. We hate the idea of losing what we have but don't necessarily act to increase whatever benefit we perceive we enjoy.

Because of their power in the organization, leaders have the responsibility and right to use these and other weapons of mass persuasion to benefit the individual and the organization. Does that mean they always should?

Don't Wear Business-Casual Ethics

On one hand, almost daily another story surfaces about an organization, a specific leader, or a politician engaging in malfeasance or unethical behavior. On the other hand, as a nation, we forgive or merely forget easily. Her supporters recovered from Hillary Clinton's e-mail problems about as quickly as Donald Trump's overlooked his latest gaffe. Companies haven't enjoyed the same fate. When 2016 headlines mentioned Wells Fargo created more than a million fake accounts, heads rolled and fines mounted. These kinds of scandals ruin the individual reputations of the company's leaders, but they also position the organization to experience years of severe damage to its reputation—influencing subsequent trust and future earnings. Companies like Wells Fargo learn the hard way that business-casual ethics may pay in the short run, but the company ends up paying mightily in the long run.

That's what happened in 2002 to a small firm of 100 employees. The owner of the company created a conflict between his employees' ethics and the ethical values of the company: "Make money, even if it means bending the rules." He encouraged employees to misrepresent services, to sell services clients didn't need, and to alter data, if that would help to retain customers. He created a highly damaging form of stress that caused significant turnover in the 100-person firm.

The average member of his technical staff earned about $100,000 per year but billed four times that. Each year one or two of these key people left, usually in response to the stress of working for this unethical boss. At the time, I estimated the firm lost approximately a million dollars a year. For a company that grossed about $10 million in revenue, this accounted for a 10 percent loss in their revenues—every year—all because the owner decided to wear business-casual ethics. He attempted to create a culture characterized by high profits but ended up constructing one that permitted and promoted dishonest business practices—and low profits. He also lost me as a consultant when I challenged a pivotal decision.

To establish and augment an organization's culture, leaders have the responsibility to teach the organization's core beliefs to employees without disrupting or challenging ethics. What does that mean? Drawing from the work of social psychologist Robert Cialdini, consider these six principles for influencing the behaviors of others ethically:

1. Reciprocity: Give to get, but give first. Make top performers want to work for you personally. If you give first—not just a paycheck but other benefits like information, service, concessions, choice assignments, or attention—they will feel obligated to reciprocate. Further, if you build a culture of reciprocity, you will find members "policing" the reciprocity. That is, a sense of fair play will emerge that demands employees show their loyalty to the company and to each other.
2. Consistency and Commitment: People want to feel consistent with what they have said and done in the past, especially when they have done it publicly. Therefore, give and elicit promises. When people write down a goal, they increase their chances of accomplishing it. When they write it down and then say it out loud to others who depend on them, they significantly increase the rate of follow through.
3. Inclusion: People frequently decide what to do in a particular situation by observing what others have done. Average employees will want to do what the high potentials do, so emphasize what everyone can do to align with the best and brightest.
4. Rapport: People respond favorably to leaders they like or respect, especially if these leaders communicate that they care in return. When leaders express their appreciation of people in the organization and point out *how* employees embody admirable behaviors, employees start to feel both included and liked, which engenders more of the desirable behaviors.
5. Authority: People frequently defer to a person they perceive as knowledgeable because doing so gives them a decision-making

shortcut and aligns them with those whom others admire. Fill your organization with knowledgeable, trustworthy experts whom others can claim as peers, and you'll soon find you have built a culture characterized by both ethics and expertise.
6. Scarcity—The Rule of the Rare: People want more of something they consider scarce. If you build an organization that hires only the best, you create a kind of exclusive "club" that others want to join. You don't offer membership to all, only those who want to work hard and do great things. Become a collector of rare performers, and you'll find your collection can outperform all others. If you communicate the exceptional nature of both your organization and your employees, you create a talent magnet—and a culture where employees can't stand the idea of losing anything to the competition.

Ethical behavior defines philosophical conditions that guide your organization—not just a set of protocols. Integrity must form the foundation of your culture and drive all other decisions, but before that can happen, leaders need to identify the beliefs and behaviors that will march in lockstep precision with ethics in all kinds of conditions.

Persuasion and Peer Pressure

In 1964, W. D. Hamilton, one of the most influential evolutionary biologists of the 20th century, introduced the theory he called "inclusive fitness." Inclusive fitness involves the number of offspring and offspring equivalents an individual rears, rescues, or otherwise treats altruistically. Hamilton showed mathematically that, because other members of a population may share one's genes, a gene can also increase its evolutionary success by indirectly promoting the reproduction and survival of other individuals who also carry that gene. This observation engendered the "kin selection" theory. As the theory explains, a gene's fondest wish is to be passed into the next generation. This occurs when the creature carrying the gene survives to reproduce. But the propensity to reproduce also occurs if the creature's relatives, who carry the same genes, survive to reproduce. This theory helps to explain why a small bird will fake injury to distract a hawk from its young, thereby acting altruistically toward its kin.

It also helps to explain how relationships not only intensify our willingness to help those we consider part of our clan, but how they also *cause* us to want to. When we share an identity with others, either through our genes or associations, we have a heightened ability to influence others, and they, in turn, have the power to influence us. It's about shared identity. Every salesperson knows customers want to buy from those they like, but not everyone understands we "buy" ideas from those we consider like us—not just those we like.

Employees who work in companies that have healthy cultures leverage this power of kinship. The more closely we share an identity with those with whom we work, the more dramatic the feelings of merging with one another.

Although peer groups, which may or may not actually be teams, continue to function as individuals, the process of group formation causes the collection of individuals to form a new entity, something that has a new, unique identity. Peer groups do not consist of mindless individuals all conforming to some preordained path to group consensus. Rather, individuals continually structure their groups through their communication behaviors. All groups, no matter how stable they appear, change with members' interactions—a process that both internal and external factors shape. These factors take on more significance when we realize people tend to help most those they consider in their in-crowd.

A series of studies by British psychologist Mark Levine indicates that, in the most extreme of cases, some things bind rather than divide us. Levine and his team asked Manchester United fans to write down what they liked about their team, which was the first step in a multistep experiment. Then they had the fans move to another building for the second phase. Along the way, they encountered a seemingly injured jogger who was part of the experiment. Sometimes the jogger wore a Manchester shirt, sometimes a plain shirt, and sometimes a shirt of rival team, Liverpool. When the jogger wore a Manchester shirt, the overwhelming majority of participants stopped to help, but few stopped to help the Liverpool jogger. The researchers concluded people have a strong tendency to help most those they see as belonging to groups with whom they identify.[5]

The British researchers determined commonalities bind us, which should not surprise anyone. But anyone who has worked in the tech world realizes that *uncommon* commonalities bind people even more intensely. For example, people who make video games offer a rare combination of talents. They are part artist, part storyteller, and part technical expert. Peers like these in a given company probably share features rarely found in other external individuals and groups. These uncommon commonalities cause peers to feel connected, and at times, to develop a them-against-us mindset for those outside the clan. This sort of bond and mindset create a bedrock on which to influence. And it doesn't take much.

In the 1990s, social scientists James Wilson and George Kelling proposed the "broken window" theory. This theory suggested that even small signs of disorder, such as a single broken window in a neighborhood that goes unfixed, encourage *more* widespread negative behavior.[6] Further related research demonstrated when people observe that their peers have violated one social norm, not only will they have the potential to violate that same norm themselves, but they are also more likely to violate a related but different norm. Further, allowing visible signs of norm violation, like a broken window, that seem relatively unimportant might elicit norm violations in more important areas.

Peers play a tricky balancing act in influencing. They can have an "everyone is doing the right thing, and you should too" inspiration, or they can overuse a good thing to the point that it stimulates negative results. That's what social psychologist Irving Janis concluded in 1972 when he first identified "groupthink" as a phenomenon that occurs when decision makers accept proposals without scrutiny, suppress opposing thoughts, or limit analysis and disagreement. Historians often blame groupthink for such fiascoes as Pearl Harbor, the Bay of Pigs invasion, the Vietnam War, the Watergate break-in, and the Challenger disaster. We now realize groupthink causes a group to make an incomplete examination of the data and the available options, which can lead the participants to a simplistic solution to a complex problem. Don't confuse "simplistic" with "simple." *Simplistic* solutions imply a naive, single-minded approach. *Simple* solutions show evidence of Occam's Razor—the shaving away of *irrelevant* information, not the suppression of critical facts or quick fixes.

High cohesion, a positive group dynamic, creates problems when the group has excessive amounts of it. When groups become too unified, the members, especially the insecure or weak ones, allow loyalty to the group to cloud their ability to make effective determinations. Often these weak participants engage in self-censorship because they perceive that "the group knows better." This, coupled with their fear of rejection and the stronger members exerting direct pressure to conform, discourages the voicing of dissenting ideas and leads to mind-guarding, which peers can develop in a highly cohesive group.

Through subtle or overt pressure, powerful peers can create an atmosphere of intolerance to dissenting ideas, which prevents the raising of objections and alternate solutions. The absence of *obvious* dissent leads peers to conclude others concur; they assume everyone agrees; and an illusion of unanimity surfaces. This process can then lead to collective rationalization, the process through which peers invent justification for their actions, causing them to feel they are acting in the best interest of the group. A "safety in numbers" mentality develops and can lead to excessive risk-taking when the group feels accountable to no one.

Researcher Robert Cialdini addressed the ways peers influence each other in his seminal work, *Influence*. According to Cialdini *social proof* provides a potent weapon of influence. This principle states that one way to determine correct behavior is to find out what other people deem correct. We view behavior as more correct in a given situation to the degree that we see others performing it.[7]

Before Irving Janis, Walter Lippmann, American writer, reporter, and political commentator, coined the word "stereotype." He wrote, "Where all think alike, no one thinks very much." In chapter 6, I advise readers not to major in the minors, but sometimes the minor things can have a major impact on peer relationships. Everyone seems to agree peers play an important and profound role in shaping behavior and influencing each other. The job of those who lead these groups of peers is to shape the environment so that positive influences can persuade people to behave in accord with what serves the group and to avoid the mind-guarding that leads to groupthink. In the 19th century, British philosopher and economist John Stuart Mill observed, "The only purpose for which power can be rightfully exercised over any member of a civilized community against his will is to prevent harm to others." The harm employees face tends toward the economic, but no one should underestimate it. Peers can help in creating a civilized community that serves to mitigate harm, even if no one can eliminate it entirely.

Conclusion

Author John Gardner wrote:

> We must learn to honor excellence in every socially acceptable human activity—and to scorn shoddiness, however exalted the activity. An excellent plumber is infinitely more admirable than an incompetent philosopher. The society which scorns excellence in plumbing because plumbing is a humble activity—and tolerates shoddiness in philosophy because it is an exalted activity—will have neither good plumbing nor good philosophy. Neither its pipes nor its theory will hold water.

Although accurate, Gardner didn't go far enough. He neglected to mention *what* we must do to embrace excellence and scorn shoddiness. Gardner overlooked, but business leaders can't afford to ignore, the role influence and persuasion must play in defining individual and organizational success.

Modern corporations don't and can't practice mind control, even if it exists beyond limited improvised settings and science fiction. Insidious attempts may exist to manipulate others, but they usually don't work too well or for too long. Successful leaders have discovered effective methods to lead others through influence and persuasion—not force. They have found ways to apply F^2 Leadership—to balance firmness and fairness to influence results.

PART II
Action

CHAPTER 6

Getting More without Settling for Less

In 1519 Hernan Cortes landed in Mexico with 600 Spaniards and 11 boats. The conquistador and his men had just embarked on a conquest of the Aztec empire, one that hoarded a cache of the world's greatest treasures—gold, silver, and precious jewels. Cortes undertook this mission knowing that for centuries other conquerors with far more resources had attempted to colonize the Yucatan Peninsula, but none had ever succeeded. Cortes changed the course of history, however, with three words: "Burn the boats."

Cortes wasn't the first man to ensure victory with a bold strategic decision, however. A thousand years earlier, Alexander the Great also burned his boats upon arrival on the shores of Persia. Like Cortes, Alexander faced insurmountable odds and an army that far outnumbered his own. He too ordered the boats burned with the cry, "We go home in Persian ships, or we die."

Conquerors tend not to enjoy a laudable place in the history books, but they do offer lessons in how to get more without settling for less. Pilots refer to PNR—the point of no return. This technical term in air navigation refers to the point in a flight at which, due to fuel consumption, a plane no longer has the capacity to return. To inspire innovation and reinvention, businesses often face a PNR too—a point in their history when they need to burn the boats that brought them metaphorically.

Companies like Kodak faced a burn-the-boats period in their history when they realized they had to switch from selling only hard products to offering digital services. Dell too "burned" their direct selling model and began selling through retailers.

In 1971, Darwin Smith took the helm of Kimberly-Clark, a paper mill company founded in 1872 in Neenah, Wisconsin. The company broadened its operation in the 1920s to introduce Kleenex, the first throwaway tissue. The company developed a system to produce coated paper and paper for books as well. Shortly after he took the chief executive position, Smith sold large interests in coated paper and closed the inefficient mills, a burn-the-boats decision that engendered appalling ridicule. With this new direction, focus on new consumer products, and cash, Smith renamed Huggies, a disposable diaper that would compete successfully with the leading brand, Pampers, and, eventually, would take the first-place position against Procter & Gamble.

Getting more without settling for less demands strong leaders who make tough calls about the direction of the company, the trade-offs required for success, and the people needed for enduring success. Leaders like Cortes, Alexander the Great, and Darwin Smith figured out what they had to do. Today, each leader must look at the unique internal and external landscape to determine what needs to happen. Only the discerning and determined will succeed.

If We Weren't Already Doing This, Would We Start?

When I ask clients that question, it prompts stunned silence followed swiftly by mild irritation (open hostility tends to emerge a few minutes later). Several minutes into the conversation, a leader of a family-owned business might mention a particularly troubling family-member employee. At that time, I ask, "If that person were not a family member, would she/he still work here?" The reaction to that question usually appears *eerily* like the original stunned silence.

Why do these leaders have a stunned reaction to these questions? Simply put, they had never thought of either question, much less either answer. They feel confused and more than a little embarrassed because they don't know how to answer the questions, and that frequently leads to annoyance. When channeled effectively, these negative feelings can give way to a brainchild. But just as physical children don't spring forth fully formed before they have finished their gestation, neither do intellectual offspring. They too need oxygen—the "airing" of ideas that breathes life into them. From these breakthroughs come invention, creativity, and discovery.

Making decisions about the direction of the company and the people who will lead it requires an application of all the constructs of tough calls. Having a competitive strategy means being different. It means *deliberately*, not capriciously, choosing a different set of activities to deliver a unique mix of value. This disciplined approach to choosing the company's direction helps to avoid what I call *organizational ambidexterity*. We know that ambidextrous people—those who can use their left and right hands equally well—comprise about 1 percent of the general population. While this trait distinguishes this group for a specific skill that we consider positive in a person, we can't say the same about organizations.

Ambidextrous organizations too often attempt to respond to the external environment with a confused strategy. They keep doing what they've always done and attempt to go a different direction at the same time—adding to the complexity of deciding which trade-offs to force and which sacred cows to kill.

In his book *The Strategy Paradox*, author Michael Raynor pointed out "a firm cannot drive its costs down while simultaneously incorporating leading-edge, and hence highly expensive, components in order to achieve high levels of performance. Therefore, minimizing cost means accepting a lower level of performance on at least some dimension."[1] Companies with this kind of ambidextrous strategy unwittingly create two areas of vulnerability. Consequently, competitors with a pure strategy can launch an attack on either flank when they discern a hybrid strategy. When leaders of a company pursuing a pure strategy face a choice, they know how to respond. They have a clear sense of their company's strategic forces, so they can coerce the trade-off decisions and avoid strategy paradoxes. In general, companies benefit when they decide to have one of four strategic forces: product development, customer needs, production capability, or method of distribution.

1. Products/Services—*What* will we sell?
    - Products or services play a key role in the future of the company.
    - Company continues to deliver products like those it has.
    - New products resemble current ones.
    - Leaders look for ways to improve products.

Examples: Car companies and Coca-Cola

Question strategists ask: "What will engineering do to improve next year's model?"

Every year car manufacturers offer their customers a newer version of the cars they have sold previously. Occasionally, but not usually, they design and manufacture a completely new product, but it still falls into the automobile category. Similarly, Coca-Cola specializes in soft drinks and develops new products to respond to demands for new flavors or diet alternatives.

2. Customer/Market Needs—To *whom* do you sell?
   - Leaders focus on current and emerging customer needs within a defined demographic.
   - Company constantly looks for alternative ways to address customer needs.
   - Needs analysis and market research determine allocation of current resources.

Examples: Fisher-Price Toys and Mayo Clinic

Questions strategists ask: "What other needs do our customers have?" and "What market do we want to serve?"

Even though toy manufacturers and health care providers may not have obvious characteristics in common, they share the same strategic force—they exist to respond to a specific demographic and the needs of that group.

3. Production Capability—How can we use what we have to make something else?
   - Capability includes the production processes, systems, and equipment to make and improve specific products.
   - New products may differ from previous products while still utilizing existing production systems and equipment.
   - The organization may make products for another organization.

Examples: A cream cheese company, a construction company, and Boeing

Question strategists ask: "Who will lease or buy our capability?"

A company that specializes in making cream cheese needs to make few adjustments to respond to new trends. This kind of company can add flavors or offer a low-fat option relatively easily. Similarly, an aircraft company that already has the processes, systems, and equipment to make planes can fairly readily adjust to a new type of plane or products for planes. But construction companies illustrate best how production capability works. A company that has the equipment and people to build an airport probably has the same production capability to build a nursing home.

4. Method of Sale or of Distribution—*How* will you sell your products or services?
   - Method of sale determines the products a company provides, the markets it enters, and its geographic scope.
   - Relationships are key to the organization's success.
   - The organization may sell products from another organization to fully maximize the method (catalog sales, for example).
   - The way products reach the customer and the systems and equipment to support the method drive this kind of company.
   - Products, customers, and geographic scope the company can handle through its established distribution channels drive this organization.

Examples: Pampered Chef, Girl Scout cookies, McDonalds, and Amazon

Questions strategists ask: "Using our existing sales force and method, what products can we offer?" "What can we sell and where can we sell it, using our existing method?"

Perhaps Avon taught modern business leaders the most about the importance of the method of sale and distribution. A team of women sold the products, door to door, to people they already knew. The only way to buy Avon required forming a relationship with an Avon Lady. Today, however, Avon has a new method of sale—they have counters in some department stores. Similarly, Tupperware relied on home parties, but, today, you'll find their kiosks in some malls. Girl Scout cookies, however, rely exclusively on their junior sales force to sell their products to people they know.

Amazon offers the most dramatic example of how a company can change its strategic focus and control its success. Initially, Amazon offered books online—a combination of product and method of distribution strategic forces. Gradually, they started offering e-books and audio books, but still mostly books in an online shopping format. Today, Amazon offers everything it originally sold, but now they also sell live video and audio streaming, not to mention every other product a consumer might desire. Its method of distribution has remained its driving force, but even the way it distributes has changed. They have truly embraced the words of their founder, Jeff Bezos, who said Amazon would be "fixed on the vision, flexible on the journey." The journey has changed several times, but his vision to sell through online shopping options has remained the same.

If you're a leader who fails to identify your strategic force and to leverage it, you may miss the trade-offs as well. In these cases, you do one of three things:

Confuse customers
Confuse employees
Engage in nonproductive activities

Tough calls related to strategy demand an answer to the question, "If we weren't already doing this, would we start?" Begin to answer that question by defining your ideal future state. That ideal perfect state probably involves improving relationships with customers, since we know 80 percent of sales are not lost to the competition—they are lost to the status quo. Too many salespeople "show up and throw up." They make the sales call and then overwhelm would-be customers with too much information about what they offer instead of gathering information about how they can help. In these situations, the salespeople resist change and create a business prevention formula that no one finds ideal. On the other hand, a company that educates/teaches its customers creates a new culture for itself and its customer. Leaders tell customers what should be keeping them up at night and then make the tough calls about allocating resources that allow everyone to sleep soundly.

Don't Major in the Minors

A regular feature at sports venues, "Kiss Cams" frame unsuspecting couples in a heart on a big screen while the game crowd cheers for them to kiss. In September 2015, Syracuse University decided to pull its kiss cam after fan Steve Port wrote to complain the common staple at sports venues "sends the wrong message at a time when colleges are fighting against sexual assault." He claimed he was just "out to raise an important issue." That's all it took—one fan with one agenda item led to the university banning an iconic sporting tradition that no one, including Port, claims ever led to bad manners, much less criminal activity.

Decision makers at Syracuse sparked outrage that we can only partially blame on Port. When they decided to remove the kiss cam, they echoed the song we have heard too many times, "Let's limit everyone's enjoyment or comfort because *maybe, possibly, someday, someone* may get hurt or have hurt feelings," or, "Let's Major in the Minors."

We see it in the safety measures at the airport, desperately and continuously attempting to assure people that somehow taking off shoes will stop someone bent on terrorism. We see it in the schools where zero tolerance of sexual assault means zero judgment when decision makers expel a kindergartner for kissing a girl. We saw it at the University of Missouri when decision makers decided all freshmen must take diversity training after a few reprobates, who may or may not have been students, shouted racial slurs from a moving truck. The university saw this as a costly but surefire approach for ending, once and for all, racism at the university. And we see it in business with more regulations and stupid rules—policies applied to the many but designed to change the behavior of the few, regulations that have no relation to or hope of eradicating the bad behavior.

When one person cheats on an expense account, abuses sick days, or generally skirts responsibilities, a new policy appears. We willingly punish 100 innocents to neutralize one troublemaker—never considering the loss of freedom to the innocents.

Majoring in major decisions requires decision makers to examine what they do, why they do it, and for whom they do it. We know products and services become obsolete or irrelevant for a variety of reasons.

1. We no longer need that product or service. Who among us wants a better buggy whip?
2. We want the new and improved version, especially in the technology arena.
3. We want more cost-effectiveness. Who still pays separately for long distance?
4. We change our perceptions, which is why clothing stores change their displays seasonally . . . or daily.
5. The provider stops providing. When did you last hear of a doctor making a house call?

We can't be all things to all people, but we can be something important to some people. Drawing from the work of Alan Weiss in *Best-Laid Plans*, consider the following adaptation:[2]

	Commodity	Increased value	Dominance
Product	Accord	Lexus	Bentley
Service	Comfort Inn	Marriott	Four Seasons
Relationship	Walmart	Nordstrom	Neiman Marcus

A product is a tangible good produced for sale. Consumers find utility in the use of the item. For example, a person can leave a store and immediately put on a shirt she purchased. But, she might also buy an insurance policy the same day—a service she hopes she *never* has to use. "Service" describes intangible value, like insurance policies, but it can also illustrate something we purchase but don't take with us, like a hotel room. "Relationship" involves the assistance we receive for no perceived fee, such as the help of a salesperson.

Companies don't grow and improve with a strategy to do things they do reasonably well most of the time. They create a competitive advantage when they determine what things they can do better than anyone else *most* of the time. The latter kind of company figures out a better way to think about the future—a way to veer away from policies and procedures to think about the direction the company should take to distinguish itself from the competition.

Drawing from your conclusions about your strategic forces, force some trade-offs. Forcing these trade-offs will typically involve doing things better or not doing them at all.

1. Refine your method of distribution.
2. Realize operational effectiveness does not serve as a substitute for strategy.
3. Delegate decisions others have shown they can make.
4. Never attempt to "coach" for more ethical behavior. Quit making excuses for underperformers.

The essential, *major* questions regarding strategy start with "why?" Why do we want to make these changes? David Maister, author of *Strategy and the Fat Smoker*, suggested more major questions:

1. Which of our habits are we *really* prepared to change, permanently and forever?
2. Which lifestyle changes are we *really* prepared to make?
3. What issues are we *really* ready to tackle?

As Maister pointed out, the necessary outcome of strategic planning is not analytical insight, but resolve. In other words, people know they need to lose weight and quit smoking. However, the rewards lie in the future; disruption, discomfort, and the discipline needed to improve are immediate. We humans don't excel at delayed gratification, but major strategy change offers little in the way of the instant variety.[3]

Achieving industry dominance demands that every key person in the organization decide *what* to sacrifice some of the present not *if* to sacrifice some of the present to enjoy a better tomorrow. This only happens when people believe their sacrifices will fuel a bigger good—a major improvement that demands something from everyone. Those who attain industry dominance know where they can compromise and where they can't.

Only when we stop majoring in the minors and responding to every malcontent with an agenda can we hope to improve our culture and our companies. Good people want freedom and will seek situations that allow them to enjoy them. We don't need to outlaw mistletoe to ensure we won't have sexual assaults any more than we need to enact endless protocols and rules to keep these good people in line. Hire ethical people and then treat them like adults. Show good judgment, and demand it in return. If you do that, you won't need a three-ring binder for your employee handbook. Just write the two words my mother said every day of my life: "Behave yourself."

What Counts That We Don't Count?

Several years ago the CEO of a large manufacturing company, Steve, asked me to help him with succession planning. Since I had just worked with the board to help them hire him, a candidate not yet 40, to fill his current role, he believed in my talent to pick the best people for key roles. But when he called me to his office, he asked for something I wasn't expecting. He asked whether I could conduct a morale survey. Any consultant with Wi-Fi can find a survey like the one he described. Similarly, anyone who can read can interpret the happy-to-grumpy scales they generate. Instead of agreeing, I asked, "How's your turnover among star performers?" He replied, "There is absolutely no turnover of any kind at this company, among any kind of performer." I pointed out to Steve that he wanted to count things that didn't count, like satisfaction with the cafeteria food. In my more than 35 years of consulting, I have never met a top performer—or any kind of performer—who cited bad food in the cafeteria as a reason for leaving. I did see the question on an evaluation form a former client asked participants to fill out after one of my training sessions, however. They too seemed bent on measuring that which doesn't count.

Counting what doesn't count costs the company in time and money. But it does something far more nefarious. It takes the focus off the things that do count, the things they should be both counting and *changing*.

Organizational change—especially as it relates to culture change—has dominated discussions since the 1980s. Theorists and practitioners argued then and disagree now about how to define it and how to measure it. Those disputes helped to create the La Brea Tar Pit of good intentions to which I refer in chapter 1.

This concept of culture and cultural change became important to leaders who wanted to understand the role morale and corporate values played in creating the environment of the company. Nearly everyone understood then and knows now that culture plays both a role in constraining change and in causing it. But few understood exactly *how* it played this role, and few agreed on what "it" was. Professor Daniel Denison distinguished himself as one of the pioneers who had a keen sense of what "it" was and is.

Denison discovered the vast nature of culture but also concluded that only some parts of a given organizational culture have relevance to what the organization needs to do. As he discovered, Edgar Schein had been right all along that a change-oriented leader cannot produce change without metrics, but a measurement-oriented leader cannot produce change without a strategy that integrates the measurement into the fabric of the change process.

Through his research, Denison learned the importance of examining both *internal* factors and *external* forces. He and his team developed a way to measure culture—a way to count what counts—in order to help organizations focus on the issues that need attention and move beyond a discussion of employee satisfaction, engagement, and morale, to better understand the decisions they must make to build organizations for the future and the actions leaders must take. He found successful organizations concentrate on their mission, adaptability, employee involvement, and consistency.

Mission includes three aspects: strategic direction, goals, and vision. *Adaptability* involves creating change, customer focus, and organizational learning. *Involvement* takes into account empowerment, team orientation, and capability development. *Consistency* considers core values, agreement, and integration. Like many models of organizational behavior, this model focuses on a set of dynamic contradictions or tensions that leaders must manage. Denison concluded effective leaders control the tension to solve two problems at the same time: external adaptation and internal integration. Every leader who has experienced a failure can tell you how relatively easy it is to influence one of the sources of tension, but success requires a leader to address several—simultaneously—in the throes of complexity.[4]

When we zero in on the critical few and put aside the trivial many, we can act on an otherwise complex decision. For example, in the 20th century people started using "culture" anthropologically to describe the range of human phenomena that cannot be attributed to genetic inheritance. It encompassed beliefs, customs, art, work, institutions, and use of symbols—the totality of socially transmitted behavior patterns. We understood the concept somewhat as it related to the study and development of human societies.

Scholars, historians, and anthropologists traditionally shied away from judgment in their description of a region's culture. They *depicted* the practices, policies, and patterns of a given people without adding editorial comment, often implying cultures aren't better or worse, just different. Well intended as this might have been, it is also wrong minded.

A few years back I commented that the New York subway system resembles a fraternity house after a toga party. I contrasted it to the Munich metro station that is cleaner than my living room. The listener commented, "There are cultural differences." No, when it comes to public transportation, Munich is better, New York worse.

The word "culture" has continued to morph as it describes organizational culture—the predominating attitudes and patterns of behavior that characterize a business. Some cultures work; others don't. Some succeed; some fail. Cultures don't merely differ. Those leaders who strive for anything other than excellence driven by integrity doom themselves and their organizations to stagnation and possible ruination.

At one time, ordinary products, services, management, and talent would have allowed you to stay in the game. Your customers and employees will reject your company if you don't create a culture that nourishes theirs. If you count what counts, you'll run through the tape at the finish line and live to enter another race. And, you'll be around a while.

Will We Be Relevant in Five Years?

Traditionally I helped clients develop one-, three-, five-, and ten-year strategies. I don't do that anymore. Companies change too quickly. Both technological advancements and their relevance to businesses change too fast, and external global forces tilt the world in unforeseen ways. Now, instead, I concentrate on the one- to three-year strategy to think about five-year results. Even the five-year crystal ball starts to fog and blur, so we formulate for the long term but plan for the short term.

In addition to setting more realistic timelines for their strategies, I encourage clients to talk about the strategy every day, in many ways, with various people. I have found most people in most companies cannot recite the company's mission statement, which seldom changes, much less the organization's strategy that changes at least partially every year. If every leader recited the strategy every day, in every meeting, after five years, everyone would have heard the strategy approximately 10,000 times (200 working days a year x 5 years x 10 times a day). This would give new meaning to Malcom Gladwell's "10,000 Hour Rule," his observation that virtuosos distinguish themselves after they have practiced at least that many hours—the approximate number of hours he discovered most had practiced to attain the level of excellence that caused others to consider them luminaries in their fields.

Knowing whether you'll be relevant in five years starts with the question of just how relevant you are right now. A well-thought-out strategic principle pinpoints the intersection of the organization's passion, excellence, and profitability, or in the case of not-for-profit organizations, its unique contribution. As you can see from the graphic, success lies at the intersection of the three.

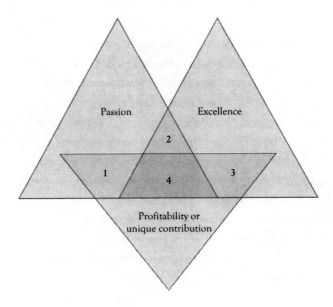

If your organization operates in Section 1—the One-Hit-Wonder section—you will probably experience some short-term success, and star performers will find themselves drawn to work for you—initially. People who do work they feel passionate about and engage in work that rewards efforts with large monetary compensation can often stay in the game for the short run. But if you aren't the best—and the clever in your organization will quickly figure out that you aren't—the competition will soon surpass you, and your best will leave you.

Section 2—the Avocational section—won't even allow you a short run. This undisciplined orientation—to do what you like and are good at—without consideration of the market, will cause your strategic vision to become nothing more than unmet aspirations.

Section 3—the Burn-Out section—eventually offers a recipe for inertia. When one is driven to *do something,* an operational bias causes quick fixes, compromises, and knee-jerk attempts to get things done. But the seductive short-term activities quickly lose their allure when you don't include passion. Star performers don't dip their professional toes into the water; they show up to make waves. If they don't feel passion for the work, they won't do it either.

The sustained success of exceptional organizations lies in Section 4—the Powerhouse section—where passion, excellence, and profitability intersect. These companies have high-quality products and services that consistently encourage them to develop newer and better offerings. Only here can your organization thrive as you work diligently to produce a product or service your competition can't match.

When companies face change or turmoil, the strategic principle acts as a lighthouse that keeps the ships from running aground. It helps maintain consistency but gives managers the freedom to make decisions that serve their part of the organization best. Even when the leadership changes, or the economic landscape shifts, the strategic principle remains the same. It helps decision makers know when to develop new practices, new products, and new markets. When they face a choice, decision makers can test their options against the strategic principle by simply applying this three-part litmus test:

- Are we passionate about this work?
- Can we do it better than our competitors?
- Will it make us money?

When designed and executed well, a strategic principle gives people clear direction while inspiring them to be flexible and to take risks. It offers a disciplined way to think about decisions, strategy, and execution and challenges people to play an ever-evolving better game. Top performers embrace both change and risk, but they do their best work when they understand the parameters within which they must work. These allow star performers to act as agents for and champions of change—rather than as mavericks or benchwarmers, the people who love benchmarks.

The term "benchmark" originated with the chiseled horizontal marks surveyors made in stone structures. They then placed an angle iron in them to form a "bench" to serve as a leveling rod. This ensured that a leveling rod could be accurately repositioned in the same place in the future.

The term started to show up in business circles in the late 1980s and early 1990s as leaders began using benchmarking to measure performance using a specific indicator (cost per unit of measure, productivity per unit of measure, defects per unit of measure, etc.) These results provided a metric of performance leaders could use to make comparisons. From these conclusions, decision makers could then determine internal "best practices." So far, so good.

Then, companies started looking outside to the competition, and industry benchmarking and best practices started to surface. The problem? The more benchmarking they did, the more they started looking like their competitors. Leaders learned that the more homogeneous your company becomes, the more you're likely to *imitate* rather than outrun your competition. This can quickly turn into a creative approach to bankruptcy.

What's the alternative? Understanding the competition can help, as long as it leads to improvement, not imitation. But too often it doesn't. An alternative approach involves looking inside your own company *temporarily* in order to look outside to the customer *permanently*.

Conclusion

We know from Greek mythology what happened to Sisyphus, the king of Corinth, when Zeus punished his self-aggrandizing trickery and deceit. Zeus condemned Sisyphus to an eternity of rolling an immense boulder up a steep hill, only to watch it roll back at him once he reached the top. We now describe laborious and futile tasks as "Sisyphean," but our attempts to get more without settling for less needn't feel like that.

We do, however, condemn ourselves and others to never-ending useless efforts and unending frustration when we continue to do what doesn't work, major in the minors, and count the trivial. Success demands new approaches.

Yogi Berra, baseball star turned philosopher, said, "In theory there is no difference between theory and practice. In practice there is." Getting more without settling for less demands we think about our companies differently and then practice the way we intend to play.

CHAPTER 7

Everybody with a Coin to Toss Is Not a Leader

The "great man" theory surfaced in the 19th century to explain leadership throughout history: Heroes possessing charisma, intelligence, wisdom, and power had created history. No theory escapes criticism, however, and detractors of this one surfaced quickly. According to critics, attributing historical events to the decisions of individuals—these supposedly "great men"—was both primitive and unscientific. As these theorists explained, "great men" were simply products of their social environments.

In the 21st century, we realize we still need great men and women, but we can't count on them to unleash their greatness in a vacuum. Instead, we need to redefine our language—to explain success not in terms of "great man" or "environment"—but by what author Thomas H. Davenport called "organizational judgment," the collective capacity to make effective decisions that exceeds the scope of any one leader's talent.

Not everyone with a coin to toss qualifies as a decision maker—at least not an effective one. It takes more. It requires us to abandon the reasoning processes that entrap us in patterns of behavior we hate but cannot seem to change. Too often these traps, based on unexamined beliefs and fears, become self-sealing, self-perpetuating, and self-sabotaging; and our best efforts to escape them merely tighten their grip. Conversely, when leaders start with exceptional decision makers and then create an environment where these decision makers can make their best tough calls, both individually and collectively, leaders position the organization for effective organizational judgment and change. They all soon learn that *un*successful decision makers focus only on the current situation. *Successful* people base their decisions on where they want to be in the future.

In chapter 7 I look back at disasters and misfortune to make sense of what happened—to clarify what leaders could and should have done to prevent negative outcomes. I challenge conventional wisdom and illustrate how congruence between espoused beliefs and operating beliefs would have led to better decisions, which would have engendered better results. Further, I explain how individuals—great and not-so-great—can lead an organization away from bad judgment and toward success.

Let's begin by defining leadership, explaining the power associated with it, and discussing the various current theories about it. That will allow us to determine where theories coalesce, collapse, and diverge.

Special Forces: People Who Disproportionately Influence Their Environments

Plato believed only a select few with superior wisdom should lead others. Aristotle contended, "From the moment of their birth, some are marked for subjugation and others for command." Machiavelli considered people weak, fallible, gullible, and dishonest; therefore, he found manipulation acceptable for achieving one's goals when the end justifies the means. He believed citizens should follow those princes who had the cunning and the ability to organize power and knowledge in the defense of the state.

St. Paul said only those deemed worthy through divine blessing could truly lead. Throughout history many believed God chose leaders through royal or aristocratic birth, and since, indeed, these men did secure positions of power, the theory remained credible. These historical perspectives haven't merely remained in the history books; they have endured to influence thinking throughout the centuries.

Different forms of this "nature/nurture" controversy continue today. Questions persist about whether leaders are born with talents and traits that allow and even cause them to succeed as leaders, or whether experience can teach effective leadership behaviors. We can't even seem to reach consensus about *universal traits* that cause leaders to be effective. Often we consider leaders intelligent, knowledgeable, attractive, sociable, and persistent; but exceptions exist.

Even the definitions of a trait differ. Trait psychologist Gordon Allport defined a trait as "a generalized and focalized neuropsychic system (peculiar to the individual) with the capacity to render many stimuli functionally equivalent and to initiate and guide consistent (equivalent) forms of adaptive and expressive behavior."[1] The theory suggested invisible characteristics exist in certain parts of the nervous system.

Another trait theorist, Richard Ryckman, viewed traits as "convenient constructs that are used to describe patterns of behaviors."[2] Clearly, a division in the ranks of the trait theorists exists, and we still have questions: Can factors of personality operate independently of one another? Or are traits elements of a person that can be used to describe patterns of behavior?

In 1948 trait theorist Ralph Stogdill tried again to provide answers when he published a review of 124 studies and surveys that had appeared in print between 1904 and 1947. Researchers in these studies identified characteristics such as initiative, social dominance, and persistence as *general* qualities of effective leaders, but, unfortunately, no common list of *specific* leadership traits surfaced then either. In fact, not only did Stogdill *not* discover a common list of leadership qualities, he also uncovered several inconsistent findings. From this search of the literature, Stogdill concluded a person does not become a leader because of the possession of some combination of traits. Rather, the characteristics of the leader must bear some relevant relationship to the characteristics, activities, and goals of the followers."[3]

What does it all mean? Clearly, considered singly, traits hold little diagnostic or predictive significance. In combination, however, they can generate personality *dynamics*, or patterns of behavior that prove advantageous to the person in a leadership role.

In chapter 5 I presented the F^2 Leadership Model to explain the *behaviors*—not skills, traits, talents, attitudes, or preferences—leaders need to demonstrate to be effective. The model sets tension between opposing forces—firmness and fairness—to provide understanding and direction. In general, the model simplifies the way we think about the dynamic and complex dilemmas that characterize leadership style. It helps leaders figure out whether they are losing balance, tending to act more like Genghis Khan or Mr. Rogers.

Both *prescriptive* and *descriptive*, the model allows leaders to understand their own behavior relative to their direct reports, but by its nature, it implies a preferred way of behaving. In other words, the model explains what leaders *should* do instead of merely describing what they tend to do or prefer to do.

As it stands, the F^2 Leadership Model offers important insights, but now I think it doesn't explain enough. My omission reminded me of a different kind of oversight: In 1975, Steve Goodman aspired to write the perfect country and western song, "You Don't Have to Call Me

Darlin'." He sent the song to his friend David Allen Coe, explaining he had achieved his goal of writing the perfect country and western song. Coe wrote Goodman back that it was *not* the perfect country and western song because he hadn't said anything about Momma, or trains, or trucks, or prison, or gettin' drunk.

Responding to the feedback, Goodman sat down and wrote another verse to the song:

> I was drunk the day my mom got out of prison,
>
> And I went to pick her up in the rain,
>
> But before I could get to the station in my pickup truck
>
> She got runned over by a damned old train.

After reading it, Coe realized his friend had indeed written the perfect country and western song and included it in the final version that fans play, usually with a beer chasing the blues away, in country bars throughout the country.

Like the nearly perfect version of Goodman's song, the F^2 Model explains the two most significant *behavioral* choices a leader must make to achieve success, but it doesn't address the *emotional* aspects of leadership, specifically the feelings that cause leaders to remain stuck in the arena of indecision and good intentions—the reactions that compromise the ability to make tough calls. So, I added another verse:

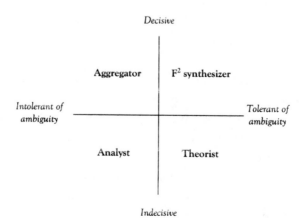

When it comes to making tough calls, the two characteristics that distinguish leaders from followers include *decisiveness* and *high ambiguity tolerance*. When people tolerate, or even appreciate, ambiguity, they demonstrate the ability to *synthesize*. From your English classes you'll recall we define synthesis as the combination of a number of different parts or ideas that produce a new idea or theory. But our memories from chemistry class would serve us better: synthesis is the production of a substance from simpler materials after a chemical reaction. The role of the leader is to serve as the catalyst for that chemical reaction.

The CEO of a large wealth management company served as just such a catalyst. He not only had a tolerance for ambiguity; I think he actually loved it. Working in the arena of investments, volatile markets, political campaigns, and the fickle finger of Wall Street, Nate would have been miserable had he not been able to appreciate the opportunities that lurked just beneath the surface at all times.

In our years of working together, I saw repeated examples of Nate embracing ambiguity. When those around him preferred to gnash their teeth, Nate remained above the fray, always willing to make a tough call once he had enough information to do so—not *all* available data, and certainly not as much information as most other leaders would require, but enough to satisfy him.

Several years ago, he asked me to assess a senior person with the idea that this man might become his replacement when Nate retires. I mentioned I didn't know they had started recruiting for a position. He replied, "We're *not*, but a guy at my golf club said we need to look at this guy and find him something to do." It ranked as the most ambiguous hiring situation in which I've ever played a part. Nate didn't have a job, much less a job description for the nonexistent position—no salary bands, no defined duties, no "package" to offer. With all the ambiguity, I thought we might have to medicate the HR lead in the office. This hiring scenario ran far afield from everything she'd been taught and held sacred. It still stands as the best hiring decision I've ever influenced.

The candidate, Dave, matched Nate in his ability to value ambiguity. They didn't aggregate data to make the decision; they *synthesized* information. They didn't act as observers of the hiring process; they created it in a way that it may never exist again. Had one or the other lacked an appreciation of ambiguity or lacked a willingness to make an unconventional call, this story would not have a happy ending. But it does. As Nate nears retirement, Dave has stepped up and stepped into the leadership role that never existed before but one they don't ever want to operate without again.

Great Leaders Versus Organizational Judgment

The situational theories of leadership surfaced in modern business circles shortly after the discussion of traits. Situational theorists denied the influences of different characteristics, attributing all variance among individuals to demands of the environment. A question began to surface. What role does chance or luck play in the rise of a leader? Would Hitler, for example, have been able to wreak such formidable havoc had he lived in a different place or at a different time?

In addition to no universal list of leadership traits existing, *behaviors* associated with great leadership show no consistency either. Behavioral theorists, such as B. F. Skinner, would have argued that leadership is learned behavior influenced by genetics but not by traits. They contend that reinforcement of leadership behaviors and punishment of nonleadership behaviors determine who will become a leader. Many behaviorists maintain that we can explain and control behaviors purely by manipulation of the environment. It follows that if we can *identify* these leadership behaviors, we can *teach* them. If leaders are made, not born, can we teach leadership only to those who already possess the innate ability to lead?

Personality theories aside, we can trace some of the confusion and disagreement concerning leadership and decision making to a failure to distinguish between "the leader" and "leadership." If nothing else, 21st-century social science research established that leadership is a *function* of group process, rather than a series of traits residing in a particular individual. Clearly, a "leader" does not exist apart from some particular group or organization. Leaders must have followers.

We now understand, in addition to ability and a situation that provides followers, leaders must also have a desire to lead. If an individual has the talent and training to lead but no motivation to work in a leadership position, success seems unlikely. Sometimes a desire for popularity or a wish to avoid stress and responsibility cause an individual to settle for nonleadership roles. Others feel motivated by needs that have nothing to do with garnering recognition.

Leaders lead because groups demand direction and rely on leaders; and while not all groups have a leader, most groups have some form of leadership. In this frame of reference, describing the "universal" leader or the "ideal" leader remains impossible.

However, describing leadership *functions* and *roles* and then discovering which members perform accordingly becomes possible. Functioning in a leadership role involves exerting *influence* and *power*. One person can play this role, or group members can share it. In most successful groups, you'll find one *recognized* leader but leadership responsibilities shared among the members.

The qualifying statement, "in most successful groups," introduces another question. To what extent do we measure the impact or effectiveness of the leader by the success of the followers? Certainly, some would immediately answer "Yes!" Losing coaches get fired; boards terminate CEOs of nonprofitable companies; and we don't elect political candidates who make poor showings at the polls. But in each of these cases, does the failure of the group imply leadership did not take place?

Who would say Robert E. Lee did not lead the Confederate forces? Would historians accuse Napoleon of *not l*eading his men at Waterloo? Would anyone argue that Hitler did not come dangerously close to realizing his goal of creating a master race? In each of these examples, the followers failed, but did the leaders? Lee, Napoleon, and Hitler led losing teams, but the history books still hail them as some of the most effective leaders of all time. Have the criteria for measuring great leadership changed? Do we now define leadership solely by successful outcomes?

There is a mystique about leaders. The definitions of leadership involve abstract, nebulous words such as visionary, charismatic, proactive, and purposeful. Describing leadership in specific, observable terms proves more difficult; and a definition eludes us. We often have an emotional reaction to the word "leader." For instance, we might say leaders inspire others to greater effort, and managers provide the necessary resources for that greater effort. Ideally, would the same person do both, allowing the inspiration and practical application to work in tandem?

Could an effective leader lack practical managerial skills? Some argue that all leaders are managers but not all managers are leaders. The lines between management and leadership blur because we define the words differently. Personal connotations overpower objective denotations. In my work with thousands of executives, I have found leadership *style*, more than leadership traits, determines a leader's effectiveness.

Not only do we not agree about a theory of leadership, some question the very notion of leadership. They believe the present emphasis on individualism and freedom of choice stands at odds with the traditional reliance on strong, effective leaders. Some people would purposefully avoid leadership because they believe it requires the manipulation of other persons and limits people's freedom of choice. These individuals tend to associate leadership with elitism and the kind of power seeking which sometimes leads to corruption of goals and unnecessary conflict.

Others would go so far as to say modern education and mass communication make leaders unnecessary. As yet, however, there has been no indication that leaders are no longer necessary, and apparently, there are no successful groups without leadership. Even when some members of a group consciously avoid leader roles, others arise to fill the void. The first question, then, remains not whether there should or should not be leaders, but what constitutes the most effective and desirable leadership for a given organization? Author Thomas H. Davenport defined organization judgment as "the collective capacity to make good calls and wise moves when the need for them exceeds the scope of any single leader's direct call." He also provided the second important question: What does a culture of organizational judgment look like?

> It's a culture of modesty and self-examination. It's a culture where people admit errors and become students of those errors. It's a culture that is deliberative—that doesn't fly off the handle but also isn't paralyzed by excessive analysis. It's a culture that figures out how long it has to make a key decision and then makes it in that time period—neither too fast nor too slow. It's a culture that uses data when there is data available. And it's a culture that values the intelligence and experience of its people.[4]

In *Competing on Analytics: The New Science of Winning*, Thomas H. Davenport and Jeanne G. Harris argued that the frontier for using data to make decisions has shifted dramatically. Certain high-performing enterprises now build their competitive strategies around data-driven insights that, in turn, generate impressive business results. Their secret weapon? Analytics: sophisticated quantitative and statistical analysis and predictive modeling.

Exemplars of analytics use new tools to identify their most profitable customers to offer them the right price, accelerate product innovation, optimize supply chains, and identify the true drivers of financial performance. A wealth of examples—from organizations as diverse as Amazon, Barclays, Capital One, Harrah's, Procter & Gamble, Wachovia, and the Boston Red Sox—illuminate how to leverage the power of analytics.

Great leaders or organizational judgment? Not an either-or situation. We need big data, analytics, organizational, AND great thinkers with big judgment to know what to do with all the facts. We need creative individuals who can put the pieces of the puzzle together, but they have to have the right pieces to start with—and the tolerance for ambiguity that allows them to synthesize. We will always need talented individuals to make sense of diverse viewpoints and data points. Otherwise, we end up with people willing to make the tough calls, but they get them wrong, and others suffer the consequences.

Bad Calls: The Mother of Unintended Consequences

The culture of the U.S. Navy changed forever as the result of the scandal surrounding the 35th Annual Tailhook Association Symposium at the Las Vegas Hilton—but the changes haven't been all good. Even though the word "Tailhook" conjures images of inappropriate behavior among civilians and others unfamiliar with it, the association exists to engender positive outcomes. According to the Tailhook Association website, "The purposes of the Association are: to foster, encourage, develop, study, and support the aircraft carrier, sea-based aircraft, both fixed and rotary wing, and aircrews of the United States of America; and to educate and inform the public in the appropriate role of the aircraft carrier and carrier aviation in the nation's defense system."[5] The 1991 Tailhook scandal refers to the actions at a specific symposium and the resulting investigation conducted by the Department of the Navy, the Inspector General of the Department of Defense, and the Armed Services Committee.

For several reasons, in this instance and many others, the military offers some of the best examples of significant cultural changes. First, leadership in both the civilian and uniformed ranks of the military changes every three or four years. The decisions that coerce change happen quickly, often driven by the deadline of a leader leaving a given position. Second, the public takes an interest in cultural issues of the military since tax dollars pay for its existence. Third, whether in peace or war, politicians miss no opportunity to flex their political muscle in all things military. The Tailhook scandal offers concrete examples of each—examples that left the reputations of many blameless, well-intended people tarnished forever and the consequences for the guilty nonexistent.

In short, those guilty of assault escaped criminal prosecution, and none of the accused officers was convicted at court-martial. But the process ruined the careers of many innocents who were either denied promotion or forced into premature retirement. Ultimately, 14 admirals and almost 300 naval aviators suffered because of Tailhook and the subsequent debacle of an investigation and efforts to force cultural change.

Thirteen years before Tailhook 1991, the air force hired me to develop programs to educate senior enlisted personnel about the challenges they would face as women began to assume more roles in the military. Throughout the Tactical Air Command, personnel at all levels received training about what to expect and what would be expected of them. The approach mirrored the programs that Social Actions leaders had implemented as more blacks began to enter the military and reach leadership positions.

On the heels of the "Love School" race relations training, the unofficial name of the initiative, gender training received about equal derision. Almost universally, people hated these programs. Even though all of us were well intended, I now question whether we improved things for women or men as much as we had hoped to. I say that because we addressed *behavior* and ignored the values that caused the behavior and created the culture of the military.

Our early attempts to advance the role of women in the military took a direct hit because of Tailhook 1991. Nothing could have damaged women's rights more than the double standards of performance and professional conduct that emerged after the incident. That is, none of the women who attended Tailhook was ever subjected to investigation for improper acts, even though significant evidence surfaced that many female participants had abused alcohol and engaged in the same questionable "conduct unbecoming an officer" that their male counterparts had suffered persecution for. The double standards of the investigation also caused resentment among the female participants' male colleagues.

How did the perfect storm of Tailhook touch down in September of 1991? The short answer is timing. In the aftermath of Vietnam, women began to take new roles in the military, and not everyone embraced the changes. Then, at the height of the Tailhook investigations, Bill Clinton took office and immediately shone the spotlight on gays serving in uniform. The climate became ripe for change and focused on traditional roles of military members, male and female.

Certainly, some long-held opinions about women in the military, in general, and women in combat, in particular, fueled the Tailhook scandal, but to settle for that explanation ignores the myriad other factors that played a role, the most significant being alcohol abuse. Prior to 1991, military cultures encouraged the use and abuse of alcohol. Consuming large quantities of alcohol and "holding your liquor" positioned men, especially aviators, in good stead. One personal friend, a devout Mormon who retired from the air force with four stars on his shoulders, received some bad advice shortly after his 1971 commission: The self-appointed adviser told him he couldn't hope to have a career in the military if he didn't drink. Obviously, my friend proved the soothsayer wrong, but we shouldn't ignore the significance of the outdated advice: At one time, everyone expected fliers to drink.

From the drinking grew other developments, some common to most military flying organizations, some specific to a particular branch. For instance, naval aviators (and some air force aviators) did "carrier landings," also known as "CarQuals," on long tables. These landings involved a participant running head first at a wet table, sliding to the end, hoping buddies would institute the "wire" or belt to hook his feet so he didn't fall off the end of the table. Damage to both the one landing and to the setting often occurred, but so did fun, camaraderie, and fond memories.

We should not underestimate the value of these kinds of activities since they fuel camaraderie and esprit de corps—two essential components of a flying culture. Learning to play the games and excelling at them brings people together, contributing to feelings of inclusion and pride. By their very nature, aviators tend to be a competitive lot, so any time one team can beat another team, an opportunity surfaces to have fun and enjoy each other's company.

Other not-so-good traditions have gone by the wayside, too. For instance, prior to Tailhook, many officers' clubs in the United States hired strippers for their "stag" bars, a practice not only excused but often encouraged. Similarly, inebriated male service members sometimes bared their genitals in these clubs. Off-color jokes, which no one would tolerate at most civilian corporate functions, peppered both the closed mess, which included only squadron members, and the open mess, which included both members and their guests.

Men shaving the legs of cooperating women at Tailhook grew in favor somewhere along the line. In fact, Paula Coughlin, the woman who started the Tailhook investigation because of the assault on her in the infamous third floor gantlet, submitted to leg shaving while in her uniform. Although leaders tolerated these behaviors, and—in the case of the strippers—sanctioned them by using club dues to pay the dancers, engaging in these behaviors at Tailhook 1991 drew reprimands and the demise of careers.

The point is, sometimes unique practices emerge in a given culture—behaviors that make no sense to anyone outside that culture. While often ill advised, most weren't illegal, and prior to Tailhook, not even considered conduct unbecoming an officer, the charge filed against attendees. Arguably, military culture changed in response to Tailhook, but not necessarily along the lines of fairness. Or, did the decisions and the decision makers change, which caused those in the culture to change their behavior?

In 1992, while working at El Toro Marine Corps Air Station, I met a marine aviator, a major who had attended Tailhook 1991. On the day investigators interrogated him about his attendance at the symposium,

I spoke to this marine and found his story both sad and outrageous. In addition to questioning him about his participation in Tailhook events, which included him watching a stripper and drinking alcohol, the investigators asked him numerous personal questions about his sexual fantasies, sexual practices, and use of pornography—all completely irrelevant to any claims of assault. The same congressmen and senators who had registered appropriate outrage at the sexual-assault allegations at the symposium conveyed no similar indignation that those who have sworn to give their lives for their country were treated worse than criminals—with fewer rights to privacy and counsel.

The military's tolerance for and encouragement of alcohol use has changed dramatically in the more than 25 years since Tailhook. Regrettably, many of the officers' clubs have closed or merged into "All Hands" clubs on military bases and air stations, causing a loss of camaraderie and esprit de corps. Appropriately, on the other hand, holding one's liquor is no longer held in high esteem, and a DUI can now be a career-ending move.

William McMichael, the author of *The Mother of All Hooks*, erred when he called Tailhook a "military culture gone out of control, a culture of self-aggrandizement and alcohol abuse and lack of respect for anyone outside of it and any woman trying to get into it." But he got it right when he observed that the investigation was:

> An overreaction of the nation's civilian leadership that has forced social changes down the military's throat—some good, some detrimental. It is a climate of political correctness that has in some cases lowered training standards, sometimes endangering others and culling morale. It all could have been handled so much differently.[6]

The baby went out with the bathwater after Tailhook 1991. Unintended consequences caused life to change for 300 aviators and 14 admirals, even though only a handful of them had been involved in the assault.

Decision makers in the Tailhook investigation could have avoided unintended consequences by anticipating likely consequences. The salient question, in these kinds of situations, should be "Why?" Why do we want to understand/change this? If the goal of investigators had been to identify those who had engaged in criminal behavior but to protect the innocent, the story would have had a better ending. Instead, they seemingly asked themselves, "How can we use this incident to change behaviors we've never liked?" Senior leaders did change some of the behaviors they didn't like but not without causing collateral damage.

Cultural change can come about as a result of a crisis—as the Tailhook scandal indicates—but that isn't the best path. When strong leaders learn from mistakes and make decisions to alter the course of events, behaviors change. It all starts with the values of the decision makers, however. When military leaders indicated that their beliefs about alcohol use had changed, as evidence by harsher penalties for alcohol abuse and a willingness not to tie professional performance to holding one's liquor, behaviors among military members changed too. Similarly, when leaders changed their beliefs about the role of women in the military, behaviors changed, and both altered results.

In the case of Tailhook, so many people who influenced decisions had their own agendas and often conflicting values. Some blame the suicide of the Chief of Naval Operations, Admiral Jeremy Boorda, in 1996 and of Coast Guard Captain Ernie Blanchard in 1995 on the flawed investigation.

Boorda assumed command in 1994 with the mandate to help the navy recover from the aftermath of Tailhook. He then faced an additional scandal in which some questioned his personal honor over the legitimacy of him wearing two Vietnam War combat medals. It was too much. He took his own life in 1996.

On January 10, 1995, Captain Blanchard addressed cadets and guests assembled at the Coast Guard Academy and unwisely chose to tell what he considered harmless jokes. After cadets and leaders at the academy expressed their displeasure, Blanchard apologized. But that did not end the story. To his shock, Blanchard found himself the target of a "criminal" probe. With some 30 years of military service at stake, Blanchard offered his resignation to save his pension benefits. It was refused. He killed himself in desperation, fearing his 30-year service career would end in disgrace, with a court-martial and loss of pension.

The *Washington Post* characterized the suicides as "death by political correctness," at least in part, due to the fallout from Tailhook. These men suffered the ultimate unintended consequence of bad decision making, but they weren't the only ones who bore the ultimate consequence for someone else's bad call. Often when we want to go forward, we benefit from looking back—back to historical tragedies like the sinking of *Titanic*—to understand how a company's culture can cause it to founder.

On April 14, 1912, White Star Line's luxury liner, *Titanic,* the largest ship afloat at the time, sank on her maiden voyage, killing more than 1,500 people. Most blame an iceberg for the tragedy, but a flawed belief system actually started the comedy of errors that caused the deadliest peacetime maritime disaster in modern history.

It all began with hubris. Bruce Ismay, the owner of the White Star Line, had built a ship that "not even God could sink," so he didn't equip the ship with enough lifeboats for all the passengers. Ismay also had an ego-induced goal to set a new record for an Atlantic crossing, so he disregarded conventional wisdom and warnings about speed limits for sailing in adverse weather conditions. Ismay pushed Captain Edward Smith to abandon protocol, sacrificing both safety and good judgment—causing historians to question whether the disaster would have occurred if the ship had sailed without Ismay aboard. Ismay survived the disaster, but Captain Smith and 1,500 others did not, creating a heartbreaking metaphor for what happens in too many organizations.

The terribly flawed belief system surfaced long before *Titanic's* maiden voyage, however. Decision makers at the White Star Line knowingly used inferior products to build the ship. Specifically, they decided to use substandard iron for the rivets that held sections of the ship together. Had they valued quality over cost savings, would the ship have sunk? We'll never know.

Continuing to cut costs of production, decision makers didn't make the walls separating the ship's sections below deck high enough, a singular decision that would have prevented the loss of the entire ship. The walls of the so-called "watertight" compartments rose about 11 feet above the waterline but not all the way to the top because White Star Line didn't want to sacrifice the room this would have taken from the first-class section.

We can't ignore a more insidious belief that influenced decision makers in the *Titanic* disaster. They considered the lives and comfort of first-class passengers more important than the safety of the second- and third-class passengers. At least we can infer that since most of those who lost their lives had neither the protection of high walls nor effective escape routes. Additionally, some of the stewards literally blocked the escape of passengers in steerage in the misguided notion that these second- and third-class passengers must stay out of the first-class sections, even as the ship sank.

In Unchartered Seas, Your Boat Must Be Strong

Beliefs reflect those perceptions leaders consider "correct." Over time, employees learn that certain beliefs work to reduce uncertainty in critical areas of the organization's functioning. As the espoused beliefs continue to work, they gradually transform into an articulated set of values, norms, and operational rules of behavior—embodying an ideology or organizational philosophy that serves as a guide for dealing with ambiguity and difficult events. The White Star Line didn't create a laudable ideology, so a flawed set of values emerged, setting the wheels in motion for the fate of the passengers and crew, who didn't realize they sailed on a ship of foolish beliefs.

A flawed belief system positioned *Titanic* for failure, but bad decision making and weak leadership ensured the catastrophe. Days before *Titanic* sailed, ships in the North Atlantic warned of unusual ice conditions. The day of the disaster, three ships, the *Baltic,* the *Amerika,* and the *California* sent warnings to Captain Smith, but he either didn't receive them or ignored them—at least six of them! Data existed, but good judgment didn't. Smith simply didn't take in new information that would have guided as he went. A veteran of the sea, his arrogance caused him to believe he knew everything there was to know.[7]

A successful culture must contain a core shared assumption that the appropriate way for an organization to improve involves proactive problem solving and learning. Therefore, leaders must ultimately make the *process* of learning—not any given solution to any specific problem—part of the culture. Once a ship has begun her maiden voyage, evidence of the learning should abound, but in the case of *Titanic,* it didn't. Decisions *not* to learn doomed her.

Because decision makers considered *Titanic* unsinkable, they developed no contingency plans. The ship didn't offer enough lifeboats for all aboard, but neither did the company train the sailors to handle disaster. Most of the lifeboats left with seats available because crew members erroneously believed they had to speed away from the ship in order to avoid being sucked down when it sank, and they couldn't deviate from the "women and children first" conviction, even as husbands and fathers of those on the lifeboats stood helplessly on the decks ready to board but preparing to die.

"Culture" represents that set of beliefs that govern behavior. We create it as we go along, sometimes consciously, often unconsciously, all the while hoping for the results we intend. However, when flawed beliefs and bad judgment combine, unintended consequences abound.

Captain Smith and his crew members couldn't respond to unanticipated consequences because they didn't know how. The White Star Line had not created an environment in which problem solving and innovative solutions seemed necessary or valued. Indeed, the company appeared to value and reward mindless following and conformity.

Some historians have called the loss of *Titanic* a "perfect storm" of unfortunate circumstances. It wasn't. Rather, it was a perfect storm of a flawed belief system coupled with ineffective decisions and damaged leadership that caused what others have more accurately referred to as an "event cascade" of mistakes and arrogance. Captain Smith told the media prior to sailing that his career at sea had been "uneventful." Since the maiden voyage of *Titanic* was to be his last—and fate would intervene to make sure that was true—he had become complacent in his leadership and decision making. He capitulated to the demands of the line's owner instead of following safety procedures he knew well. Similarly, he relied on unseasoned sailors with insufficient training to handle communication and rescue efforts.

One tough call could have saved *Titanic:* "Slow the ship." But Smith didn't make that call. Smith could not have anticipated all the things that would go wrong the night of April 14 any more than leaders in any organization can foresee all the problems they will encounter on a given day. An iceberg didn't sink *Titanic*; a culture of greed, hubris, elitism, and acquiescence to ignorant authority did.

Conclusion

Defining and explaining leadership, its theories, and its controversies remains a monumental task. We must consider so much—psychology, history, sociology, religion, and business. We can feel overwhelmed. The search for answers continues, and the questions continue to change too. Plato, Aristotle, Machiavelli, and St. Paul might not agree with current theories, but new thought leaders would probably force them to reexamine some of their conclusions. The changing global economy will require great women and men to do the same. Those with big data will continue to make their mark on organizations, but we still will need those with *big judgment* to sort through it all to make the tough calls.

PART III
Results

CHAPTER 8

Change Yesterday's Dangerous Ideas

No one has better personified British author Richard Dawkins's idea that yesterday's dangerous idea is "today's orthodoxy and tomorrow's cliché" than our 35th president, John Kennedy. When President Kennedy took office in January of 1961, the thought of trying to land a man on the moon terrified most rational people. Yet, the president put a stake in the ground, determined that the United States would win the space race against the Russians and would land a man on the moon within 10 years. In July of 1969, more than a year shy of the goal, we turned Kennedy's "dangerous idea" into reality.

Space exploration quickly morphed into orthodoxy as we funded more space travel and set new and challenging objectives. Missions like Apollo 13 and other mishaps gave us pause and caused us to continue to see space travel as dangerous, but not too many years passed before we started to take launches for granted. I hope they never become clichés, but they have become commonplace because decision makers continually and consistently demanded the United States be first, fast, and fantastic.

Organizational change, the double-edged sword, can build a technology giant like Apple, but it can also unleash a backlash or unrest and turbulence. Researcher James O'Toole addressed the emotional side of change when he wrote about "the ideology of comfort and the tyranny of custom," pointing out that a status quo mindset does more than create a philosophy; it establishes a risk-averse, oppressive dogma that quashes new ideas, novel approaches, and innovation.

Intellectually, business leaders understand they must champion change to keep pace with, let alone outrun, their competition. Yet, people often feel trapped by their own ideology, acting as though an oppressive regime or organizational structure has been forced on them by an unknown agent. They see themselves as victims, but they aren't. They themselves have created their own traps and tyranny by making the status quo resistant to change. Imprisoned by their own behavior, they avoid conversations that would help them discover the gaps between their intention to change and their decisions to change.

Where does the balance between honoring the company's history and embracing the future occur? When does a stake in the ground serve as a sign of commitment, and when does it tether the warrior to his or her grave? We need to understand the advantages of change and the pitfalls of getting it wrong. Only then can we address the tough calls leaders must make to serve as agents for change while preserving the best of what should *never* change.

What's the Smallest Change We've Made That Had the Biggest Impact?

Too often people think of change as a stellar opportunity to lose control of their lives, not as an exciting occasion to improve them. They sacrifice themselves on the altar of custom when they imagine change in broad, sweeping terms and allow their fears to tyrannize them. When these fears surface in the leaders, a wrong-headed approach to innovation permeates the organization like a cancer. Successful leaders take a different approach. They walk toward change as Gladiators walking into an arena, hearing the crowd chanting their names. They realize drastic change seldom works as well as steady, incremental change.

These organizational gladiators also never underestimate the value of the short-term win. They know real transformation takes time, and without the small victories along the way, people can lose their focus and sense of urgency, which leads to them feel defeated.

The most successful companies don't allow their competitors to define the playing field. Instead, they challenge themselves to see opportunities their competitors don't see. They redefine the terms of competition by embracing one-of-a-kind ideas in a world of copycat thinking. They look two years out and ask what will be different—both the challenges and the opportunities. They then ask the important question: How can we position ourselves to be ready for that new playing field?

One of my most successful clients asked that question recently. In a world where the lowest bid usually lands the deal, leaders at this construction company realized they needed new ways to distinguish themselves from the competition—new ways to stand out. They accomplished this goal by researching new financing options for their clients, making it easier to get money for the project, which made it easier to do business with my client. The same client realized they couldn't be merely "pretty good" at everything anymore; they had to become the *best* at something, so they improved their hiring processes to bring on board strong decision makers who could more readily and effectively solve problems that hadn't existed before.

Eventually, every successful company has to determine how to become the best at something: the best value for the money, the best customer service, or the best quality. Companies used to feel comfortable in the middle of the road—that's where all the customers were. Today, the middle of the road is the road to ruin. You have to distinguish yourself in some way, and you can't be all things to all people.

Do an assessment. What specific parts of your company offer the best of something? Who in your firm is an industry expert?

When I work with companies on a strategy or change initiatives, I begin by asking them, "If your company went out of business tomorrow, who would miss you and why?" The answer frames the discussion about what small changes will ensure the company retains customers while it looks at changes to bring new customers in the door.

Your unique contribution to the world defines the ways you must be alert to opportunities to change. What technology/changes to process/services/intellectual property will we need to add? What steps must we take to retain our unique edge?

These steps usually lead to answers about how to use the company's history to define its future. Leaders figure out ways to use what they already know to go beyond what they already think and do.

The most creative leaders I've met don't disavow the past. They apply previous learning and experience to new situations. They see patterns, so they know what to keep and what to discard. They don't advocate change for its own sake. Rather, they rediscover and reinterpret what has to come before as a way to ignite and foster innovation.

They also learn quickly. They realize they must keep pace with the rate at which the world changes. In a world that never stops changing, great leaders must never stop learning. How do you push yourself as an individual to keep growing and evolving—so your company can do the same? How can you commit to discovering the small—often daily—changes that have the most profound results? Often the answer lies in looking back at what has defined success for the company up until now. Nothing fuels energy and succeeds like deconstructing success. When people take the time to examine what they've done and why it worked, they learn what they need to do *next* time—even though the same situation won't show up in exactly the same way.

We know from our accounting classes, if we invest a dollar, in 72 days we'll double our money. The same applies to business. If we invest the time and resources to make small changes, in a short time, we will compound interest (pun intended). It all starts with identifying both the strategic and tactical small changes that will have big results.

Are You Tough Enough to Cross the Rubicon?

During the Roman republic, the river Rubicon marked the boundary between the Roman province of Cisalpine Gaul to the northeast and Italy proper to the south. The river distinguished not only the geographic boundaries for the province but also the military restrictions for governors and magistrates. Therefore, rulers required generals to disband their armies before entering Italy, and if a general entered Italy while exercising command of an army, both the general and his soldiers became outlaws who automatically faced death.

In 49 BC, Julius Caesar led a single legion south across the Rubicon from Cisalpine Gaul to Italy on his way to Rome. In doing so, he deliberately broke the law and made armed conflict inevitable. Historical accounts of the event depict Caesar approaching the river, as he uttered the famous phrase, Alea jacta est (the die has been cast), an act of insurrection and treason.

The phrase "crossing the Rubicon" has survived to refer to any individual or group committing itself irrevocably to a risky or revolutionary course of action—the point of no return. In organizations, crossing the

Rubicon need not involve treason or even revolutionary behavior. Rather, it means making the decision to innovate, to depart radically from the status quo, or to take the risks you've been avoiding. Once the "die has been cast," why do change initiatives still fail? Change usually fails for one of 10 reasons:

1. Most people in most organizations can't recite the company's mission statement, much less articulate an ideal future state for the organization, so they don't understand why a change should happen.
2. Leaders show a reluctance to make the tough call that the change needs to happen and will happen. They spend too much time "vetting" the decision in a feeble attempt to get buy in. Too much deliberation usually just frustrates people and delays the needed change.
3. Leaders lose sight of the macro, concentrating too much on the micro—too much focus on tactics and activities and not enough on long-range goals.
4. Leaders fail to serve as either champions of or agents for the change, communicating that they will comply, rather than commit, to the change. I advocate robust debate about major changes to an organization, as long as those debates take place behind closed doors. Just as children don't want to hear their parents fighting, employees don't want to witness discord among senior leaders.
5. Too many people have an exaggerated concern about the disruptions that may happen in the short run instead of optimism about future gains and rewards.
6. People develop a propensity to fix current symptoms (to problem-solve), which only restores circumstances to the status quo, ignoring innovative decision making.
7. The focus turns inward, and people take their eyes off the customer.
8. Managers hesitate or fail to delegate specific areas of the change initiative to individuals, and withhold the authority and responsibility it would take to make the requisite decisions.
9. Leaders fail to hold people accountable for results.
10. Senior leaders have a misguided notion that they know what will happen in five years, which can build either a false sense of security or a sense of dread among employees.

With the Gallic Wars concluded, the Senate ordered Caesar to step down from his military command and return to Rome. He refused. Instead, Caesar marked his defiance by crossing the Rubicon, illegally entering Roman Italy under arms, causing a civil war, and engendering a victory that put him in an unrivaled position of power and influence. While in power, he assumed control of the government, centralized the bureaucracy of the Republic, began programs of social and governmental reform, and created the Julian Calendar.

Boldness defined Caesar's change initiatives and success, but so did risk—risk that ultimately led to his demise. Fortunately for most business leaders, even rebellious employees won't be allowed to assassinate those with whom they disagree—not even on the Ides of March.

What to Expect When You're Expecting Change

Centuries ago, a two-part, seemingly contradictory pictogram from the Chinese language indicated an understanding of why people resist change. The bottom part of the symbol meant "opportunity"; the top character meant "danger." To the ancient Chinese, change included part danger, part opportunity. (Caesar probably would have agreed.) This ancient symbol helps explain why people have long resisted change or have become immobilized by it: They fear change will bring more danger than opportunity. The Chinese knew this centuries ago, and 21st-century leaders realize it every day. People don't really fear the change *itself*; rather, they fear the loss it might bring. Children don't fear the dark; they fear what might lurk in the dark. Employees don't differ.

Change, or transition, involves *movement*, a process that occurs in a series of steps. Sometimes change happens instantly, and the steps happen almost simultaneously, as they do during a crisis. But more often, change occurs over time and involves a transition from one state to another—a predictable process that occurs as people go through the stages of change, as they do with a succession plan.

Researchers and theorists have defined these predictable stages. Kurt Lewin described three phases: unfreezing, movement, and refreezing. My research with the Vietnam POWs indicated they went through three major stages that I call Awareness, Adjustment, and Readiness to move forward. Typically, we go through these same three stages when a change occurs in our lives, regardless of the change. If we adapt, choose to go through the stages in a purposeful way, and earn the rewards of mastering the challenges the change presents, the three stages become our stepping stones to success and empower us to move toward triumph.

Just as we can learn to empower ourselves and move toward success, we can also learn helplessness. Angry or resistant, we imagine ourselves victims of change. We get stuck in one of the stages, and the stages become a progression that leads away from happiness. Leaders who want to keep the best and brightest people engaged can benefit from understanding these stages of change so they can help those in their chains of command triumph.

When change comes into our lives, we can react in one of two ways: We resist, or we adapt. Similarly, when leading others, you can help them with their reactions to change by managing your own responses more successfully. Often you won't initially champion a change that circumstances or people have imposed on you. You might feel angry; you may be scared; you might even feel immobilized. But whatever your initial emotions, if you can put them aside, you will be better able to help others with their own feelings. This control occurs only when you better understand the change and when you go through this stage with a sense of clear-eyed optimism instead of head-down denial.

Stage I describes the period when we become aware of the change. Sometimes the awareness happens suddenly and unexpectedly; at other times, we see it coming, and it arrives more gradually. During Stage I employees will need you, the leader, to act as a true change agent—or at least pretend to be one. You will need to extend reassurances and support to encourage your direct reports to accept the change, whenever possible. Presenting accurate and complete information offers the surest way to reduce anxiety at any stage of the change process, but it is particularly crucial during the initial phase. Explaining timelines, processes, rationale, and any other factors will help ease people through this difficult time.

Too often leaders relegate that communication to human resources or assume upper management will take care of it. In reality, communication must be *your* priority. Your direct reports will look to *you* for answers, so try to provide as many as you can as often as you can. If you don't attend to this function of your job, rumors will run rampant, and the grapevine will hum with damaging information or misinformation. Be consistent, clear, and endlessly repetitious.

We find trust hardest to establish when we need it most—a paradox we often find surprising and disturbing. In times of change, we foster trust in the usual ways, but then we add two more constructs: predictability and consistency, two things that are in short supply during a transition. Your direct reports will look to you to provide both, however. As much as possible, they will want you to let them know what to expect and to reassure them that, no matter what happens, things will be okay.

After we deal with the initial surprise, disappointment, or delight of awareness, we enter Stage II: People begin to accept that, like it or not, the change will not go away. During this period, people accept the unavoidable nature of the change, even if it came more by imposition than by invitation. During Stage II, we all face new choices: either build obstacles to resist the change or cope and explore opportunities. Even if they didn't skate through the first stage too well, after several weeks or months, people start to live in harmony with their changed world. They may still need help, however, to make wise decisions to reinvent their worlds, or they may be tempted to retreat from coping.

Once they have had a chance to adjust to their new circumstances, most people show both a willingness and readiness to identify new goals and to focus clearly on how to reach them. Having experienced the transformation of transition, they are ready to commit. Reaching this stage doesn't happen automatically, however. Sometimes people get stuck in a previous stage, and the change will not be successful for them. However, most people won't regress; they will want to commit and adapt.

Leading Through the Stages

How can leaders help those in their chains of command move through the stages? During the Awareness stage, if people react with a sense of adventure and opportunity, you won't have to do too much except listen to their ideas. However, if they respond with denial, you will need to be more involved. First, make sure you communicate your own acceptance of the change, even if that feels somewhat forced and counterfeit in its early stages. Next, ask open-ended questions that will help people discover what they want to do:

What are some options for making this easier?
What opportunities will we have now that we wouldn't have had before?
How might you take an active role in this transition?
What might you gain personally from this change?

Keep in mind that no matter what you do, this will be a tough time for many people. An old expression rings true: "The only people who like change are wet babies." While not universally accurate, there is some veracity in the conclusion that people may want variety and change, but they also want to feel some control over it. When they don't, they can end up feeling helpless and hopeless.

The length of time it takes most people to go through this stage will vary greatly. Some will breeze through in a matter of days, but more typically, people will need a few weeks to let the reality sink in. If people become mired here for more than two months, there may be significant issues at play that will require more help than a leader can offer. Winston Churchill offered some sage advice for people going through Stage I: "If you're going through hell, keep going."

The next stage, adjusting to a new reality or a new set of realities, requires the development of new skills or the honing of skills so they can be applied to a new set of circumstances. Specifically, your direct reports will need your help with problem-solving, relationships, and flexibility, the same three skills you will need for yourself to maintain altitude, airspeed, and ideas.

Problem-solving involves the ability to deal directly with the difficult situations we face and to make positive changes to resolve them. Effective problem-solving includes critical thinking, a global perspective, strategic planning, and the ability to anticipate consequences. When you eagerly probe for understanding, go beyond the obvious, and prioritize effectively, you will help your direct reports see the future as open and malleable—not threatening and rigid. Together you will be able to paint a credible picture of opportunities and possibilities and to communicate your enthusiasm for making them happen. You can help others cope with change by improving their problem-solving abilities.

Encourage them to solve problems as soon as they become aware of them. If they can break down problems and manage each facet individually, they will avoid feeling overwhelmed. Don't let them get trapped into thinking only *one* solution exists. See options as having pros and cons rather than being "right" or "wrong."

Open communication, the single most important skill during a transition period, will help your direct reports build relationships and share thoughts and feelings with you and with each other to promote mutual understanding. Those who welcome closeness will have developed a supportive social fabric in each area of their lives. When they combine effective communication and closeness, they will have the necessary tools for building relationships. That will help them stay connected and supported during difficult times, but these connections don't happen automatically. On the contrary, the closeness that engenders effective communication relies on a willingness to listen—your willingness and theirs—the capacity to convey respect for others' ideas, and a genuine interest in people. When they exhibit these behaviors that make them feel close to each other, they will have the trust and safety to engage in fun, laughter, and play. A sense of what is funny, or mirth, has its basis in the individual, but the true value of humor manifests in interpersonal associations.

Making *relationships* a priority, building time into our lives for the people who are important to us, laughing together, and having fun with each other all create interactions characterized by joy and fun. Sharing our feelings and concerns enhances these relationships and encourages more closeness. An upward spiral of cohesion and connection starts to build on itself when we communicate with one another in our attempts to focus on the positive. As a result, we deal with the stressors in our lives better. You can't force these kinds of things, however. You can only create an environment in which they can flourish. During times of change, the wise leader does well to realize people will need to spend more time building a sense of connection to people both at home and at work.

Flexibility describes the degree of organization in our lives and the extent to which we feel comfortable with unstructured and unpredictable situations—the ambiguity that surfaces most profoundly during times of change. Life is unpredictable, so our responses to the problems it creates need to be too. Mental agility has another important payoff: It stimulates creativity. Being open to a variety of creative and imaginative alternatives allows us to avoid getting trapped into thinking we have only one possible resolution. When you encourage your direct reports to avoid rigidity in their thinking, to experiment with innovation, and to seek the input of others, they can become more open to new ways of solving problems.

Once you help people quit fighting the currents and you learn how to flow with the people, they can approach decision making with new dexterity and energy. No one can control change, yet if we're not careful, it will control us. When people feel forced to adjust to new, uninvited changes, they feel out of control—a common, normal response.

As the Vietnam POWs taught us, finding humor in difficult situations is one way of controlling what we can control, even if we don't have power over the events that required us to marshal our coping behaviors in the first place. As explained in chapter 4, much evidence supports the conclusion that humor plays an important role in our resilience. People have learned to rely on it, not in spite of crisis, but *because* of it. Becoming aware of the value of using humor to expand coping behaviors can increase our understanding of the powerful role humor and laughter can play in helping us bounce back from the hardships unwanted changes often bring. Then, consciously and actively working to help others find humor in their daily lives can help them *feel* better until things *get better*. When we use humor to tackle problems effectively, build strong relationships, and explore new ideas, we are doing what we can do to turn challenges into opportunities. Even though the second stage of adjustment may take your direct reports two or three months, with your help, they will be ready to move forward.

Offering ongoing support during Stage III will keep people moving in the right direction. If you see regression, take it as a sign the person never really coped with the change. You might see an attempt at moving forward, but if you sense no real progress, this might be an indication the person needs more help. Sometimes too many changes that come too close together can cause people to regress. At other times, changes in the personal lives of your direct reports may seemingly gang up on them. Whatever the cause, leaders do well to react in the same responsive way. Determine what people are experiencing, and then offer them the guidance and support they need, provided they will let you. To do that, consider the E's of Change approach:

- Exemplify the behavior you desire, and don't allow yourself to feel like a victim. As the leader, you'll need to demonstrate that you support the change. If the change will happen anyway, and there's nothing you can do about it, do your direct reports a favor and keep your concerns to yourself. Voice your reservations to your boss, the board of directors, your friends, your spouse, or your minister, but spare your direct reports. They need *your* help; you can't rely on them for their help.
- Engage your direct reports in two-way communication that fosters trust and conveys respect for their ideas. Listen to feedback and consider concerns. The absolute last thing your direct reports need is a boss who, in essence, says, "Tell me what you need, and I'll tell you how to get along without it." People will have subjective, illogical reactions to unwanted changes, so they will need you to listen empathically and help them sort out what they need to do. Remember, what you *say* will only be a part of engaging others. The best sermons are *lived*, not *preached*, and the most important words you say will be whispered, not shouted.
- Energize yourself and others by keeping a clear sense of purpose for the change. Create a safe learning environment for experimenting with any new procedures. Consider the lines from A. A. Milne's classic, *Winnie-the-Pooh*, so you can help yourself and others avoid a similar fate:

Here is Edward Bear, coming downstairs now, bump, bump, bump, on the back of his head behind Christopher Robin. It is, as far as he knows, the only way of coming downstairs, but sometimes he feels that there really is another way, if only he could stop bumping for a moment and think of it.

- One of your responsibilities includes helping your direct reports quit bumping for a moment so they can explore new, better ways of thinking. The path to their problems' solutions may seem to be littered constantly with risks. Only when you concentrate on confronting problems squarely and learning from failures can everyone focus on identifying and removing obstacles to everyone's success—the bumps in your world. For learning to take place, candor is crucial and patience remains key.
- Educate yourself and others about the change. Talk about *why* not just *how* the change has occurred. Have an achievable goal in mind, and clearly communicate it to everyone affected. Through one-on-one discussions, memos, emails, group presentations, and reports, disseminate the facts. Your candor will go a long way in reducing resistance. Gather as much data as possible. Let the facts speak for themselves, and then deliver information to everyone whose life and work will be affected.
- Elevate your processes. Move from mere problem-solving to innovation. Involve others early in the process and, if possible, use a committee or team to help with the implementation. You may solve some problems by calling on those in the trenches. As Taoist sage Lao-tzu put it, "Learn from the people. Plan with the people . . . . When the task is accomplished, the people all remark 'We have done it ourselves.'"

When possible, measure outcomes and report progress. Even if people have initially defied the change, once they understand how the new conditions will help the organization, they will likely accept that they stand to profit too. Whenever possible, reinforce the change by demonstrating the relationship between their behavior and organizational success.

What Prevents Us from Making Changes We Know Will Work?

The simplest explanation for why people resist change is that they fear more danger than opportunity. They see the change as unwanted, unknown, and unnecessary. Usually change involves loss, even all they lose is predictability or familiarity. Change often creates emotional overload and chaos, two of the most potent ingredients in the recipe for resistance. We oppose change when we don't have confidence it will work, when we feel threatened, when we had no input in the decision, or when we just liked things the way they were. People who violently oppose change can create culture traps to contain, compromise, or control it.

Why do people engage in behaviors that are counterproductive to their own stated objectives? Why do they deny they do that? And why do they deny they are denying? Fear causes people to develop the "victim mentality" to which I referred earlier. They begin to feel helpless—and the emotion can take on epidemic proportions. Soon, you'll find these people showing an unwillingness to face conflict and unpleasant situations because they fear even more loss. At all costs, they want to avoid threatening and embarrassing situations.

That's what has immobilized Mitch who owns a small company he inherited from his father. Mitch has enjoyed huge success, more than doubled the business he inherited, and has grown the business by adding both new products and new clients. He knows what he has to do to enjoy more success, but he won't make the tough calls that will bring about the change. He has the experience, judgment, and moral compass, but he lacks fortitude. He holds other people responsible for his failure to change and overlooks his own responsibilities.

When I confront him with his indecision, he says, "I know. This is driving me crazy," and then doesn't call me for six months. He has every reason to believe he knows what will work, and I tell him he does, but he still won't act. He has good intentions but fears consequences. He ends up with unintended consequences but doesn't always see his pattern. His ego plays a role in his frustration, too.

You'll find ego involvement with the status quo often prevents us from making changes we know will work. We look back and attempt to justify the decisions that created the status quo instead of examining new evidence that might cause us to change our minds. We lie to ourselves and others, saying what we decided *then* was the only thing that could have been done. This sort of self-fueling defense mechanism convinces us that our action represented a brilliant solution at the time. From that, we build defensive arguments that we should keep things as they are *now*.

Self-justification stands at the heart of cognitive dissonance—the mental stress of those who hold contradictory *beliefs* at the same time or who act in discord with their own beliefs. In his book, *Organizational Traps*, Chris Argyris called this the engine that drives self-justification, the mental discomfort people experience when others question their reason and falsify their predictions.[1] We humans strive for consistency and abhor dissonance, so we take steps to ensure the former and eliminate the latter. This can lead to Machiavellian—the end justifies the means—actions that cause us to avoid any information that might inflict further discomfort. During times of change, successful leaders recognize they must comfort the afflicted and afflict the comfortable, but this requires herculean self-awareness, discipline, and restraint.

Others don't make the changes they know will work simply because they have a strong risk aversion. They don't like to gamble and want definitive, objective evidence that no part of the change can fail. Few change initiatives offer this sort of guarantee. When these people can't find the 100 percent reassurance they desire, they develop pessimism and question whether they ever believed the change would work. They also lack fortitude but try to mask this fact by claiming the need for more analysis.

The sort of pessimism that surfaces during planned change takes on the characteristic of a poverty mindset. Instead of recognizing that they have everything they need to make the changes, they doubt they will ever have enough—enough data, enough resources, enough control, enough talent, or enough strength—to make the tough calls, even when deep down they know they *can*.

Doing what you know will work requires all the constructs of tough calls—experience, moral gyroscope, judgment, and fortitude—but it demands more. Our moral gyroscope must compel us to *demonstrate* our integrity. We do not create integrity in a time of change or crisis, but we do reveal it. When we do, we not only know what will work; we do something with the knowledge.

Want to manage resistance successfully? Prepare for it. Leaders frequently focus their attention on the abstract process of the change instead of carefully listening to their direct reports about the practical problems that they will encounter in their altered worlds. Too often leaders overlook the fact that change requires new behaviors, new ways of thinking, and new set of practices or protocols.

When people know the 4 P's of change, the **P**urpose of the change, the **P**icture of what it will look like, a **P**lan for going forward, and the **P**art they will play in the new system, they begin to move toward success. When a major change occurs, discuss what decisions each person will have in the new world. If people feel that they have a say, they will commit to results. However, empowerment does not mean abandonment, and delegation does not mean abdication. Giving people permission to do something differently is not helpful if they can't do it.

Conclusion

John Steinbeck said, "Change comes like a little wind that ruffles the curtains at dawn, and it comes like the stealthy perfume of wildflowers hidden in the grass." Change may come to individuals like that, but in most organizations, the change is more like a tornado than a gentle wind. Demands of the marketplace, the accelerating pace of globalization, innovative technology, and new alliances—all have created needs for leaders to help their people respond quickly and repeatedly to change. Some people thrive on change; they have trouble when things become too predictable or mundane. Those individuals will need your ideas for developing and challenging their talent. However, this chapter addresses the change-averse or change-challenged. This not-so-silent majority would prefer a root canal to any change in their software. To help them, therefore, you'll need to understand how to manage change and its impact on people—one of the most fundamental aspects of leadership.

The rapidity of change and the multifaceted nature of it have created situations for which most of today's leaders have not prepared. The popular leadership models that for so long provided formulae that equipped leaders to solve business problems have been inadequate and insufficient in today's world because the great thinkers who tested them did so in an age of slower change that no longer exists. Today the orthodoxies of mainstream change endeavors may not be enough to keep your people productive and engaged when they didn't welcome the change. Yet, in spite of the daunting complexities and uncertainties, we ask leaders to be the heroes and dynamic geniuses that will keep the doors open and the till full.

Managing change is a demand of leaders, the avoidance of it its antithesis. For centuries people have understood that the ability to know when to take risks, revolutionize, respond, and adjust separated those who succeeded from those who did not. Hundreds of years ago, Dante provided a warning to the leader who might be tempted to think otherwise. He described hell as "the miserable way taken by the sorry souls of those who lived without disgrace or without praise." Unlike hell, however, risk, change aversion, and the mediocrity that both often engender will not last an eternity. Those leaders who do not adjust and adapt both themselves and their organizations will quickly leave the competitive arena. Successful leaders will take their places.

CHAPTER 9

What Motivates Us to Make Tough Calls?

Not for the first time, we are seeing a gap between what science knows and what business leaders do. Science has carried out extensive experiments on mice, monkeys, and humans to reach conclusions about what makes us tick. Psychologists, too, jumping on the motivational bandwagon, offer reasonable explanations about why humans behave the way we do. These theorists often overlap and build on one another's ideas, but just as frequently, they *disagree*. We expect more from science! We want someone to develop a blood test or chest x-ray that allows us to "have a look" at how much motivation a person has. We want to measure it so we can control it. Neither option exists, however.

Motivation moves us to action, but it does more. A kick will cause a dog to move, but we shouldn't infer the canine experienced any kind of intrinsic motivation to act. Rather, it wanted to avoid pain. Human motivation tends to be more complex. Humans act because we have evolved natures and myriad social, cultural, religious, and family influences.

Why do people behave the way they do? Why do wide variations in behavior exist? Why do some people have trouble making tough calls while others don't? Attempting to answer these questions has kept social and behavioral scientists busy, but clearly no one has reached a definitive conclusion. Each investigator offers a different perspective.

In chapter 9 I offer insights to bridge the gap—to examine how once-motivated people can lose the desire to learn and change in a climate that doesn't nurture those behaviors. A non-nurturing climate can cause once-motivated and never-motivated people to join forces—as much as inertia can be described as a force. They quit making tough calls because they don't see the point. What good does it do? They feel like victims trapped in a mental hospital, so they often flee the asylum, taking their expensive training, experience, and expertise to the competition. This chapter also offers alternatives—options for creating a learning environment where bright people create and don't get bored.

Let's Start with a Psychology Lesson

Even though expounding on possible reasons for human behavior has occurred for centuries, psychology is a relatively new science. It emerged as an independent scientific discipline in Germany during the middle of the 19th century and defined its task as the analysis of consciousness in the normal adult human being. Psychologists set the goal of discovering the basic elements of consciousness and determining how these elements formed what they called compounds.

Different camps began to argue the main function of the mind, or consciousness, has to do with its *active* processes rather than with its *passive* contents. Others argued that the private, subjective nature of the human mind doesn't lend itself to investigation. Sensing, not sensations; thinking, not ideas; imagining, not images—these *actions* should be the principal subject of psychology, according to proponents of this point of view. Sigmund Freud's attack came from yet another direction. He asserted we need to study the *un*conscious to make sense of human behavior.

Freud constructed a "tip-of-the-iceberg" theory that likened the mind to an iceberg in which the smaller part showing above the surface of the water represents the realm of consciousness, while the much larger mass below the water level corresponds with the realm of unconsciousness. This vast, deeper domain, Freud maintained, contains the urges, passions, repressed ideas, and feelings that exercise control over our conscious thoughts and deeds. Freud, a *psychodynamic theorist*, assumed conscious and unconscious conflicts that go on inside a person developed the personality and explained a person's motives. He considered limiting analysis to consciousness wholly inadequate for understanding human behavior.

In Freud's opinion, conflicts often occur between the conscious and unconscious and among the components of each. We humans, therefore, continuously and inevitably find ourselves in the grips of a clash among opposing forces. Life becomes a compromise that involves a dynamic balance of those forces—the three components of the mind: the id, the ego, and the superego. According to Freud, conflicts arise as the three systems of the mind compete for the limited amount of psychic energy available, energy that has its starting point in the instinctual needs of the individual.

Sometimes the *id*, the "seething cauldron" rooted in the biology of the individual, motivates our behavior—behavior that consists primarily of urges, primitive desires, and unconscious sexual and aggressive instincts. This amoral part of the personality does not concern itself with the niceties and conventions of society.

Freud realized people do not exist in a vacuum, however, and fitting into a society requires the individual to control impulses. As Freud explained, the *ego* forms to provide direction for impulses when a person's needs require interaction with the environment. While the id causes us to concern ourselves only with satisfying pleasure, the ego mediates between the instinctual drives of the person and the conditions of the surrounding environment.

The *superego* provides the moral part of the personality that tries to inhibit the impulses of the id, especially sexual and aggressive ones. The superego persuades the ego to substitute moralistic goals for realistic ones, to represent the *ideal* rather than the *real*, to strive for perfection, and to consider right or wrong, not just practical or pleasurable. Freud called the ego the battlefield where the "armies" of the id and the superego continually clash.

Carl Jung joined Freud in the study of the unconscious and in the development of the psychoanalytic theory. Jung, however, ultimately rejected many of Freud's perspectives and created his own explanations about what motivates us. While Freud stressed the *inherited* forces that shape personality, Jung emphasized *environmental* factors. Jung maintained that *aims* as well as *causes* govern a person's life.

According to Jung, both individual and racial history (cause) and aspirations (purpose and design) affect behavior. In Jung's opinion, then, a person's ancestral history plays a part in determining personality, but this combines with other forces to paint the whole picture. The environment changes the individual, but in part, predispositions guide and determine what an individual will become conscious of and respond to.

We might consider Jung on the psychological fence when it comes to the nature/nurture question about what motivates us.

Critics find Jung's theory vague, inconsistent, and complex. Additionally, in proposing a theory of archetypes and collective racial unconscious at a time when Hitler dominated discussions about a master race, Jung drew criticism for appearing to sympathize with the Nazis, an accusation he vehemently denied.

Scientists have more recently become interested in testing some of the theories, however, and we feel the impact of Jung's work today. He introduced the view that people express four basic functions: thinking, feeling, sensing, and intuition. We use these dimensions to classify people according to their problem-solving orientations. The Myers-Briggs Type Indicator, which has become a respected and valuable tool for many organizations, emerged from Jung's theory about psychological types.

Erik Erikson, a German psychoanalytic psychologist, continued the work of the earlier psychoanalytic psychologists. Students of group behavior have a particular interest in Erikson because he focused on *identity*. He suggested we develop our identities from the groups we join: family, church, school, and professional peers. Clearly, Erikson has been a vanguard in the study of organizational culture and diversity awareness.

Two major perspectives shaped the course of psychology. The first concerned itself with the study of causes, origins, or reasons for behavior. These theorists, primarily medical doctors, attempted to find ways to cure patients—not just to explain them.

The other major school of thought, conversely, had its roots in the experimental laboratory. These researchers focused on a scientific understanding of the learning process. They assumed most people acquire or learn their behavior, and the task of the psychologist is to specify the environmental conditions responsible for producing behavior.

B. F. Skinner, whom I mentioned previously, found himself in the second camp—the one that theorized all motivation comes from a person's interaction with the environment. Skinner disputed the idea that idiosyncratic learning history and unique genetic makeup of the individual account for personality development. He described an individual as a unique organism—one who has *acquired* a repertoire of behavior—not as the originator of that behavior. Skinner pointed out individuals don't share the same genetic endowment, and, without exception, no one has identical personal histories. Hence, no two people will be motivated in precisely the same ways by precisely the same things.

Skinner studied motivation by concentrating on the learning of a multitude of behaviors that allow the individual to survive and prosper in transactions with the environment. Skinner recognized people learn throughout life which situations provide pleasure and which produce pain. All personality theorists emphasized surviving and prospering, but we see a division in the ranks about whether we learn the skills for prospering, as Skinner suggested, or whether we acquire these skills through our innate natures, as the humanists would challenge.

Most of the preceding investigators, in some way, influenced Abraham Maslow, one of the leading humanists. Most humanistic psychologists tend to see themselves as *opposed* to behaviorism and psychoanalysis, but Maslow included these psychologies in his approach.

Maslow developed what we call the self-fulfillment theory or self-actualization theory. This *health psychology*, as Maslow called it, offered more possibilities for explaining why people behave the way they do. His ideas quickly became popular because, finally, someone wanted to study the behavior of psychologically healthy people to learn more about the growth process. Maslow assumed most of what motivates us is our quest to satisfy our biological, safety, inclusion, respect, and self-actualization needs.

Frederick Herzberg built on Maslow's theory. Conduct an employee-engagement survey, and you'll learn about infuriating bosses, low salaries, bad work conditions, annoying coworkers, and bothersome rules. Managed badly, these environmental factors annoy people and even demotivate them. But even when you remove those factors or manage around them, "fixing" the situation doesn't motivate people. Instead, Herzberg discovered sidestepping the demotivators provides a beginning—but only a beginning. Savvy leaders must do more; they must hire highly motivated people and then make decisions that allow these high achievers to achieve.

Herzberg's groundbreaking theories influenced a generation of scholars and managers, but they never truly penetrated corporate America, if the extraordinary attention still paid to compensation and incentive packages is any indication. Turf battles continue for extended periods without resolution, and those caught in the crossfire despair. In meetings, people nod their heads in agreement and then rush out of the room to voice complaints to sympathetic ears in private—unmotivated to improve their performance and disgusted with the leader's inability to make the tough calls that would improve their lives. Herzberg's ideas helped but not enough.

Now, Let's Dispel Some Myths

One of the most striking myths about motivation involves the inaccurate assumption that if we can "read" people and situations, we know ourselves too. And, if we know ourselves well, we will understand what motivates us. Mark, a senior sales leader at a large company certainly thought so. He prided himself on his ability to size up a sales situation quickly and to close the sale faster than anyone could. Mark took more interest in *why* people did what they did than in *what* they actually did. He enjoyed the complexities evident in human personality, motivation, and behavior. Not always practical in his approach, he succeeded nonetheless in keeping his pipeline humming. He closed more deals than anyone else at the company and quickly rose to the top where the company expected him to oversee the success of other salespeople. Instead of his psychological insights serving him well in his new role as sales leader, they served as a pebble in his psychic shoe. He felt the constant nagging feeling he had missed something, but he couldn't identify it, even though, up until *then* he could zero in on what *exactly* caused sales to soar or tank.

In our work together, I assured Mark he wasn't losing his touch. He still understood how and why sales happen, and he had a fairly firm grasp on what motivated his sales team. He just didn't understand what made *him* tick. He lacked self-awareness. He possessed the four constructs of tough calls—judgment, a moral gyroscope, experience, and fortitude— and he understood how they applied to others, but he hadn't figured out how to relate this knowledge to himself in his new role.

He required more. He needed to understand better how to harness his passion for selling and derive the same satisfaction from leading *others* to more impressive sales goals that he felt with his own accomplishments. He didn't understand how changes to his role had changed the environment from one where he did his best work to one where he felt his motivation wane. He failed to discern patterns in his behavior, so he also overlooked the effect he had on others.

Mark dispelled an important myth—the one that says "motivation comes from within, so there's little a leader or other outsider can do to influence it." Not so! Most people consider themselves self-aware, just as most people consider themselves good drivers, but judging from the number of auto accidents every year and the number of failed business ventures, we must challenge *those* myths too. Often, in fact, usually, most people most of the time need a trusted adviser to help them identify their sources of motivation and to discover how to make more satisfying decisions. Only with feedback do we see our behavior objectively, so only then can we take steps to behave in ways that reveal our motivation.

But that leads to another myth—the one that encourages us to believe we can create motivation out of nothing. Just as we can't create energy, we can't create motivation, at least not in others. We can guide it, encourage it, hone it, and destroy it, but we can't create it. For years, I have advised clients to hire motivated people and then avoid *de*motivating them.

Also, avoid falling into what I call the "generationalism" trap. This myth encourages us to believe that the year of our birth determines our motivation. In your chain of command, you may have baby boomers, gen-Xers, some members of generation Y, and some millennials. Authors fill books with advice about how you must manage and lead the people in your organization, based solely on the year of their birth. Apparently, according to those authors, you will automatically understand all those who share your generation but remain flummoxed by those who don't.

People who would never dream of engaging in sexism or racism don't hesitate to jump on the "generationalism" bandwagon. But before you invest your time in learning more about the generations, consider this: Bill Gates, Bill Clinton—baby boomers. Tom Hanks, Michael Jordan, and Jay Leno, also baby boomers. Osama bin Laden—a baby boomer. Can somebody tell me what common motivator drove the decisions of these men? If this much diversity exists in this short list of baby boomers, doesn't it make sense that uniqueness and variety exist within each generation in your organization too?

Explaining how generations differ in their motivation—or how gender, race, and religion affect motivation—offers lazy leaders an excuse not to explore the unique constellation of factors that motivates the decisions of those in their chain of command. Aside from wasting your time studying a never-proven theory about generational differences, you will engage in biases that will certainly stand in the way of you identifying your stars. Top performers know no generational, gender, race, or religious distinctions. They do share three traits, however: They are smart enough to do the job; they are driven to do it well; and they have integrity.

The most insidious motivation myths encourage us to stereotype—to conclude we can pigeonhole people the way we would sort pieces of mail. It's not that easy. We must realize the uniqueness of individuals in order to understand, much less influence, how they behave.

For instance, some people find a fast-paced workplace stimulating and challenging. Others consider it debilitating and scary. Some find interaction invigorating; others consider it exhausting. One person might do her best work when situations require her to think on her feet; another person may prefer to plan things carefully. Some have a keen eye for the details and the motivation to dig painstakingly for understanding; others regard detail work as torture.

We can infer people's motives from patterns of behavior, and we can use this information to create an environment where they can do their best work. But beyond that, we can't control what motivates a person or whether an individual will be motivated in the ways we would prefer. We can, however, try to keep them engaged.

Boredom: The Enemy of Motivation

When I screen applicants for hiring or promoting, I often detect parts of what motivates them. When I encounter a person with a high IQ, strong analytical abilities, and well-honed quantitative skills, I know I have met someone who learns quickly. Good news. But people who learn quickly also tend to bore easily. Bad news. Once they master a task or solve a puzzle, they want to move quickly to the next challenge. If the scope of their job doesn't allow for this kind of advancement, they either stick around with depleted motivation, or they take their newly acquired training and knowledge elsewhere. They quit making the tough calls simply because they don't see what good they will do, and tough calls become less tough with experience and augmented judgment.

Smart people *love* making tough calls. Their drive to figure things out keeps them engaged and focused. The higher the stakes, the better. The more uncertain the outcome, the more fun the decision. Of course, not all smart people relish the chase. Some prefer a deliberate, systematic approach to decision making. They want to weigh options, hear differing points of view, and base their decisions on definitive information, not guesswork or probability. This kind of person often finds routine tasks, like accounting, rewarding. These kinds of people *don't* bore so easily, even if they do learn quickly. Their leaders don't need to worry too much about job enrichment.

The bosses of the other kind of smart person to whom I refer do need to ward off boredom, however. Herzberg taught us the opposite of job dissatisfaction is not job satisfaction but *no* job dissatisfaction. He also taught us ways to enrich the jobs and therefore stimulate the motivation of this kind of person. Herzberg advised the following:

1. Remove controls while retaining accountability. This will allow people to take responsibility for their work and provide feelings of accomplishment.
2. Give a person complete assignments, not pieces of a larger one. This allows for the intrinsic rewards of achievement and external recognition.
3. Grant job freedom. When delegating tasks, also delegate both the responsibility and accountability for making all the tough calls associated with completing the task.
4. Introduce new and more difficult tasks as the person shows proficiency. This will stimulate intrinsic rewards.
5. Allow people to become experts. Nothing is more self-actualizing than the feeling of being the hero. When others turn to this person for advice and direction, a positive cycle of action, recognition, and more action occurs.[1]

Achievement: The Third Drive

My sister and I grew up in the same house, same culture, and same time in history. We have the same parents, wore the same clothes, and attended the same church. We look alike and share many of the same interests, yet we find different things motivating. We both have demanding jobs, hers as an ICU nurse manager, mine as a consultant. Our jobs differ, but our needs to unwind at the end of the day are eerily similar—just not identical.

I enjoy doing crossword puzzles. As a former English teacher and an avid reader, I enjoy language and solving puzzles that use words. Mary Pat, who earned a perfect score on the math section of the SAT, finds numbers relaxing, so she does the Sudoku puzzle. We receive neither a reward nor a punishment, yet each evening will find us engaging in our recreational puzzle solving. Why? What motivates us to pursue these activities on a regular basis, when psychologists have assured us we do things to seek reward or to avoid pain? Or, as Freud pointed out, for love, work, or the love of work? A third drive must make us do these kinds of things that don't pass conventional motivational litmus tests—a drive to accomplish and to receive the emotional rewards of a job well done.

In the 1940s, Harry Harlow, a professor of psychology at the University of Wisconsin, formulated the theory of a third drive while working with rhesus monkeys. By the time Harlow started his work, theorists generally accepted that two main drives powered behavior. The first, the biological drive, causes humans to eat when hungry, drink when thirsty, and copulate to satisfy carnal urges.

While the biological drive came from within, the second drive came from without—the rewards and punishments the environment delivered in response to certain behaviors. But Harlow and his team stumbled upon something else.

The researchers devised a puzzle that required the monkeys to do three things: pull out a vertical pin, undo a hook, and lift a hinged cover. They placed the puzzle in the cages of the monkeys to observe how they would react. Something unexpected happened. The monkeys began playing with the puzzles, apparently trying to figure out what to do. To the surprise of the researchers, even though solving the puzzle did not lead to a reward, and no punishment occurred if the monkeys didn't solve the puzzle, the primates kept at it, determined to figure things out.

No one taught the monkeys how to remove the pin, slide the hook, or open the cover. No biological need or reward/punishment explanation made sense either. Harlow concluded we needed a new theory to explain this third drive: the drive to perform a task for the pleasure of figuring it out. My sister and I do our nightly puzzles for much the same reason the monkeys solved the puzzles: We enjoy it. Accomplishing a task has its own intrinsic reward—which leads to intrinsic motivation.

At first, Harlow thought the other two drives would subordinate this third new one. Of course, he theorized, if the researchers *also* rewarded the monkeys with raisins, they would see even more motivation to solve the problem. Yet, when Harlow tested this idea, the monkeys made more errors and solved the puzzles in *less* time. This body of research certainly flew in the face of conventional wisdom!

Harlow encouraged more investigation on this idea of a third drive, but then he himself abandoned this exploration and moved on to other kinds of research. However, one of Harlow's fellow researchers, Edward Deci, drew from the work with rhesus monkeys to develop self-determination theory. Deci observed intrinsic motivations are not necessarily externally rewarded. Nonetheless, they sustain passion, creativity, and sustained efforts. The interplay between the extrinsic forces acting on persons and the intrinsic motives and needs inherent in human nature is the territory of self-determination theory.[2]

Those of us who aspire to understand human behavior can't afford to ignore either intrinsic or extrinsic factors. We must honor those fundamental aspects of a person's makeup that drive behavior. We need to understand the core drivers that explain why a tired woman solves a puzzle instead of engaging in a more passive activity like watching television. Similarly, we need to understand how these inherent, deep-seated factors interact with the external world. As it turned out, conventional wisdom qualified as neither conventional nor wise. It was controversial. Deci and those like him forced us to rethink why we do what we do, even when it put him at odds with fellow psychologists.

Deci, more than other theorists, has the most to offer those of us who want to understand why some people make tough calls and why others don't. He let us understand some people simply *want* to crack puzzles and solve problems. We disentangle information the way we used to unscramble Pick-Up Sticks as children. As Deci discovered and explained, much of what we believed—like money buys performance and loyalty—just wasn't so. But most leaders in most organizations still haven't accepted this new understanding about what motivates us. They continue to talk about pay-for-performance initiatives and other kinds of extrinsic rewards instead of exploring how to leverage a person's intrinsic needs to do a good job. This outdated carrot/stick chauvinism can do more harm than good.

Why Carrots and Sticks Don't Motivate

In 2016, Wells Fargo fired more than 5,000 employees who learned the hard way carrots don't work—at least not in the long run. Beginning in 2011, leaders at Wells Fargo attempted to motivate bank employees to increase the number of accounts they opened. It worked . . . but not exactly as planned. Employees opened more than 1.5 million unauthorized bank and credit card accounts in their customers' names and charged them hundreds of thousands of dollars in fees. Decision-makers tied a substantial piece of their employees' compensation to steep sales targets and made reaching them a condition of continued employment. They saw movement, if not true motivation. Things indeed changed.

In the end, the bank paid $185 million in fines, thousands lost their jobs, the repute of the bank suffered, and new business dropped precipitously. Even when launched with the best of intentions, research and anecdotal evidence show carrots-as-motivators, like the one at Wells Fargo fail. Incentives designed to spur workers to do their best can push them to engage in unethical behavior—to do their worst.

As much as carrots don't work, we shouldn't conclude sticks-as-punishment work any better. We have centuries of evidence that punishment does not even *deter* crime, much less motivate, good behavior. In fact, when public executions existed in Europe decades ago, researchers observed crimes actually increased. How bizarre that a person witnessing the execution of a pickpocket would engage in the very crime for which the criminal faced execution! Obviously, punishment acts as a deterrent in that the person who is incarcerated or executed no longer has the capacity to commit the crime, but not even the fear of these penalties seems to reduce crime.

Ask any parents of teenagers how well punishment or even threats of punishments work. "You're grounded," the dreaded words every parent hates to utter and every teen can't bear to hear, end up punishing the parents who have to stay home to guard a sulking teenager who learned nothing from the punishment and developed only the motivation to avoid the punishment, not to engage in anything productive.

Recently a very upset client called to ask my advice about an urgent situation. One of the project managers in his chain of command had accidentally backed into a post while driving a company vehicle. The HR policy was clear: The driver must fix the damage and receive two days off without pay. Never mind that the project manager had a perfect track record of performance and spotless safety record. Rules are rules.

My client explained the problem of his direct report. The project manager needed to finish a critical part of a major project for an important client. His taking two days off would jeopardize the timeline for the project, cause enormous legal problems, and alienate a good customer with whom they hoped to do business again. In this case, the threat of punishment didn't deter the project manager from hitting the post. He never intended to. It didn't even motivate him to be more cautious. He thought he was being cautious right up until the moment of impact. Instead, all the good intentions of writing policies and creating rules backfired: The project manager felt unsupported and unappreciated for all the previous stellar work he had delivered, and he felt angry he couldn't finish the job to the customer's satisfaction.

If carrots and sticks don't motivate, what does? What causes us to do the right thing, even when doing something else would be easier, more fun, or more lucrative? Usually our integrity moves to the front of the line in these situations. When we violate our own code of conduct, we punish ourselves with guilt. Sometimes the fear of that guilt will cause us to avoid the problem behaviors, but I hesitate to say it motivates us to behave right. Usually something else plays a role.

For instance, in 1980 I taught British Literature at Villa Duchesne, a Catholic girls' school in St. Louis, and earned the whopping sum of $9,000, which was based on having a master's degree and several years of experience. As low as this figure may seem by today's standards, it represented a significant increase over the $6,000 salary I received my first year of teaching in a public school on the Mexican border several years prior.

The tuition at the girls' school was $2,000 in 1980—an amount I imagined only the wealthiest could afford. Yet, that tuition didn't cover the cost of hiring substitutes for teachers who called in sick. We got sick at about the same rate that everyone does, but we hesitated to call in because we knew the principal would ask others to cover our classes. We all had a full schedule, so volunteering to cover someone else's class put an unwelcome burden on a person's friends—the other teachers who stepped up.

Today, absenteeism continues to present problems for St. Louis public school teachers, even though they earn twelve sick days a year and two personal days, which amounts to almost three full weeks of paid leave per teacher. Most of us at Villa didn't take even *one* sick or personal day during the year, even though we wouldn't have been penalized if we had, and there was no reward if we didn't. So, what explains the difference? It must have to do with our motives.

Teachers' unions negotiate contracts that guarantee days off for each teacher. It's nothing personal. *They*, some unidentified entity, pay for the sick days of teachers who have benefits. No relationship exists between the teachers who decide to use a sick day and the faceless creatures who cut the paychecks. No one calling in sick inconveniences a friend by asking for a favor. It's the job of someone working in the school district to find a substitute, and a budget some other faceless person oversees pays that substitute. It's not personal, and in many cases, it's not even human.

Reward and punishment didn't play a role in our motivation at Villa. We wanted to do the right thing, so we let our integrity guide us. Then, we respected and valued the relationships we had built with each other, so we didn't want to do anything to tarnish them. Maslow would say our need to feel included motivated us to behave ethically and professionally, and I suspect he would be right.

Leaders who use carrots and sticks often approach their tough calls with good intentions. They imagine their strategies will promote good deeds, restrain unproductive behavior, boost creativity, and generally improve things. If we believe the results of the Wells Fargo disaster and the St. Louis public school teachers' absenteeism problem occurred because of some planned carrot/stick approach to motivation, we might also believe these methods not only don't work; they don't explain our motives for doing things. In his book *Drive*, Daniel Pink identified what he called "The Seven Deadly Flaws" of carrot-stick decisions:

1. They can extinguish intrinsic motivation.
2. They can diminish performance.
3. They can crush creativity.
4. They can crowd out good behavior.
5. They can encourage cheating, shortcuts, and unethical behavior.
6. They can become addictive.
7. They can foster short-term thinking.[3]

Extensive research has assured us tangible rewards not only don't motivate; often they can have a substantially negative effect on intrinsic motivation. When external forces—parents, schools, athletic teams, businesses—focus on the short term and attempt to control people's behavior, they can do considerable damage, counterintuitive as that might seem. Motivational researchers Deci, Koestner, and Ryan concluded, "People use rewards expecting to gain the benefit of increasing another person's motivation and behavior, but in so doing, they often incur the unintentional and hidden cost of undermining that person's intrinsic motivation toward the activity."[4] Some studies have suggested that, rather than always being positive motivators, rewards can, at times, undermine rather than enhance self-motivation, curiosity, interest, and persistence.

Rather than focusing on rewards and punishments, leaders do better when they concentrate more on how to facilitate intrinsic motivation—to build on the motivation people brought in the door on their first day and to try not to demotivate those once-motivated people. Carrots and sticks don't work, but we know that interesting work, challenges, fun, and the opportunity to work with other motivated people do.

Conclusion

Comedian Ron White once said about his arrest for public drunkenness, "I had the right to remain silent, but I didn't have the ability." Too often we find people in organizations who have the right and ability to make tough calls, but they lack the motivation. In some of these cases, we discover people who would make more tough calls more often if they worked in an environment that encouraged them to learn and take chances. But fear of making a mistake cripples them, leading to indecision.

Comparing the major theories of personality and describing the similarities and differences of each provides a beginning for discussing the major controversies of the field. Psychologists haven't embraced any one theory, and we don't even have a common list of dimensions of personality—much less one for explaining what motivates us. The nature/nurture debate continues with added and complex elements surfacing with each new theory.

The dispute about whether the past or present has a more profound effect on behavior also remains unresolved. Investigators disagree about the uniqueness of the individual versus the uniformity of the species. Some theorist drastically conflict, and others build on each other. However, studying these varying perspectives provides an inkling about human behavior, for from such inklings come answers.

APPENDIX

Your Tough Call Quotient— Your TCQ

On a scale from 1 to 5, with 5 meaning you strongly agree and 1 meaning you strongly disagree, rate the following:

Fortitude

I take appropriate risks.	1 2 3 4 5
I embrace innovation and change.	1 2 3 4 5
I focus more on improvement and growth, not on cutting costs.	1 2 3 4 5
I'm a high-energy go-getter.	1 2 3 4 5
I "leave money on the table" if the project isn't a good fit.	1 2 3 4 5

Judgment

I disregard unsolicited feedback.	1 2 3 4 5
When I'm 80 percent ready, I move. I don't need perfection.	1 2 3 4 5
I quickly separate critical issues from unimportant ones.	1 2 3 4 5
I prioritize well and, when necessary, force trade-offs.	1 2 3 4 5
I respond well to surprises, even unpleasant ones.	1 2 3 4 5

Experience

Once I make a decision, I refuse to second-guess it.	1 2 3 4 5
I'm confident that no matter what happens, I'll figure it out.	1 2 3 4 5
I am more eager to deconstruct success than to point fingers.	1 2 3 4 5
I bounce back quickly from failure and setbacks.	1 2 3 4 5
I weigh options and make decisions quickly.	1 2 3 4 5

Moral Gyroscope

I don't put up with "work around" solutions.	1 2 3 4 5
I don't tolerate mediocre performance in myself or others.	1 2 3 4 5
I willingly seek the advice of trusted advisers.	1 2 3 4 5
I address conflict directly and immediately.	1 2 3 4 5
There are no "off-limits" topics with me.	1 2 3 4 5

90 to 100: F^2 Leader

Congratulations! You're tough enough. You consistently show a great capacity to look ahead, to define purpose and direction, to coordinate the activities of others, and to support the organization's strategy. Direct reports, peers, and other leaders value your firm but fair leadership style because you not only get things done, you do so in a manner that motivates the people around you. Your balanced leadership style brings out the best performance in others, and accounts, in a large part, for your success. You challenge others to deliver their best; you stay focused; and you demand excellence. You allow the situation, not your own mood or tendencies, to determine the degree of forcefulness you use.

80 to 89: Fair but Not Firm Enough

You don't have trouble making the day-to-day decisions associated with your position, but when you face a particularly unpleasant or unpopular decision, you have difficulty. You prefer to lead by influencing and persuading, and that usually works for you. But you can experience guilt or anxiety in high-stake or crisis situations. You can enjoy success at most levels in the organization, but to move to an executive position, you'll need to improve your TCQ.

70 to 79: Accommodator

You tend to give in too easily, even when you're pretty certain you're right. Therefore, too often you gloss over conflicts, ignore troubling facts, or give in for the sake of harmony. Leaders who can't make tough decisions or who won't give negative feedback fit into the accommodator profile. You are pleasant to work for and often engender affection and loyalty, but when the results are tallied, you fall short. Unless you increase your TCQ, you will probably stall in your current position.

Below 70: Solo Contributor

You find leadership responsibilities burdensome. You tend to be cautious, unassertive, or submissive. You often drag your feet on decisions, like to take your time in accomplishing a task, and avoid changes that will cause upheaval in your life. You don't want criticism, so you avoid decisions that might trigger it. You may want the benefits of a promotion, but be careful about accepting one. You may find you're not happy when circumstances force you to make tough calls.

About the Author

For more than 35 years, senior leaders have relied on Linda Henman, PhD, to help them make tough calls. Known as *The Decision Catalyst*™, Linda advises senior leaders and boards of directors when they face essential decisions about strategy, succession planning, business growth, and mergers and acquisitions. Some of her major clients include Tyson Foods, Emerson Electric, Kraft Foods, Boeing Aircraft, Estee Lauder, and Merrill Lynch.

Through thousands of hours of consulting with hundreds of corporate clients, Linda has seen what others haven't seen, helped clients remove obstructions, and influenced decision-makers to move from merely good to brilliant.

Linda's other works include the following:

The Magnetic Boss: How to Become the Leader No One Wants to Leave
Landing in the Executive Chair
Challenge the Ordinary
Alan Weiss on Consulting
Contributing editor of two editions of *Small Group Communication: Theory and Practice*

Notes

Chapter 1

1. Diamond (1999).
2. Schein (1992).
3. Walsh (2011).
4. Blinder (2015).

Chapter 2

1. Diamond (1999, p. 174).
2. Maslow (1971, pp. 47–48).
3. (California task force) www.oac.cdlib.org/findaid/ark:/13030/kt8b69r98n/
4. Baumeister, Smart, and Boden (1996). Relation of Threatened Egotism to Violence and Aggression: The Dark Side of High Self-Esteem.
5. Seligman (1990, pp. vi–vii).

Chapter 4

1. Fine and Hartman (1968).
2. Frankl (1984, p. 63).
3. Frankl (1984, p. 84).
4. Ford and Spaulding (1973, pp. 340–43).
5. Halyburton (1989, p. 1).
6. Gaither (1973, p. 48).
7. Plumb (2014).

Chapter 5

1. Gilbert (2007, p. 24).
2. Gilbert (2007, p. 25).
3. Schein (1961, p. 18).
4. Schein (1961, pp. 284–285).
5. Levine, Prosser, and Evans (2005, pp. 443–453).
6. Wilson and Kelling (1982, pp. 29–38).
7. Cialdini (2007, p. 116).

Chapter 6

1. Raynor (2007, p. 53).
2. Weiss (1994, p. 112).
3. Maister (2008, p. 6).
4. Denison (2012, p. 7).

Chapter 7

1. Allport (1937, p. 295).
2. Ryckman (1985, p. 194).
3. Stogdill (1948, pp. 35–71).
4. Buchanan (2013).
5. The Tailhook Association (2017).
6. McMichael (1997, p. 325).
7. Nilsson (2012).

Chapter 8

1. Argyris (2010, p. 77).

Chapter 9

1. Herzberg (2003, p. 27).
2. Deci, Koestner, and Ryan (2001, pp. 1–27).
3. Pink (2009, p. 57).
4. Deci, Koestner, and Ryan (2001, p. 9).

References

Allport, G.W. 1937. *Personality: A Psychological Interpretation*, 295. New York, NY: Holt.

Argyris, C. 2010. *Organizational Traps*, 77. New York, NY: Oxford University Press.

Baumeister, R.F., L. Smart, and J.M. Boden. 1996. "Relation of Threatened Egotism to Violence and Aggression: The Dark Side of High Self-Esteem." Psychological review 103, no. 1, p. 5.

Blinder, A. 2015. "Atlanta Educators Convicted in School Cheating Scandal." www.nytimes.com/2015/04/02/us/verdict-reached-in-atlanta-school-testing-trial.html?smid=tw-bna&_r=0

Cialdini, R. 2007. *Influence*, 116. New York, NY: HarperCollins Publishers.

Deci, E., R. Koestner, and R. Ryan. 2001. "Extrinsic Rewards and Intrinsic Motivation in Education."*Review of Educational Research* Spring 71, no. 1, pp. 1–27.

Denison, D. 2012. *Leading Culture Change in Global Organizations*, 7. Hoboken, NJ: John Wiley & Sons.

Diamond, J. 1999. *Guns, Germs, and Steel*, 157. New York, NY: W.W. Norton.

Fine, P., and B. Hartman. 1968. "Psychiatric Strengths and Weaknesses of Typical Air Force Pilots." Unpublished paper of USAF School of Aerospace Medicine, Aerospace Medical Division Brooks AFB, TX.

Ford, C., and R. Spaulding. 1973. "The Pueblo Incident." *Archives of General Psychiatry* 29, pp. 340–43.

Frankl, V. 1984. *Man's Search for Meaning*, 63. New York, NY: Washington Square Press.

Gaither, R. 1973. *With God in a P.O.W. Camp*, 48. Nashville, TN: Broddman Press.

Gilbert, D. 2007. *Stumbling on Happiness*, 24. New York, NY: Vintage Books.

Halyburton, P. 1989. "A Search for Meaning." An Unpublished Paper Presented at the Mountain Empire Conference on hostages, prisoners of war, and Holocaust Survivors, p. 1. Johnson City, TN.

Herzberg, F. 2003. "One More Time: How Do You Motivate Employees?" *Harvard Business Review*, p. 27.

Leigh, B. 2013. "How Organizations Develop Good Judgment." *Inc.* May 14. www.inc.com/leigh-buchanan/thomas-davenport-q-a.html

Levine, M., A. Prosser, and D. Evans. 2005. "Identity and Emergency Intervention: How Social Group Membership and Inclusiveness of Group Boundaries Shape Helping Behavior." *Personality and Social Psychology Bulletin* 31, no. 4, pp. 443–53.

Maister, D. 2008. *Strategy and the Fat Smoker*, 6. Boston, MA: Spangle Press.

Maslow, A. 1971. The Farther Reaches of Human Nature, 47–48. New York, NY: Penguin Books.

McMichael, W. 1997. *The Mother of All Hooks*, 325. London, UK: Routledge.

Nilsson, S. 2012. *The Man Who Sank Titanic*. Gloucestershire, England: The History Press.

Pink, D. 2009. *Drive*, 57. New York, NY: Penguin Group.

Plumb, C. 2014. "Who Packed Your Parachute." www.youtube.com/watch?v=JqtUlMA3Jqo

Raynor, M. 2007. *The Strategy Paradox*, 53. New York, NY: Random House.

Ryckman, R. 1985. *Theories of Personality*, 194. Monterey, CA: Brooks/Cole Publishing Co.

Schein, E. 1961. *Coercive Persuasion*, 18. New York, NY: Norton & Company.

Schein, E. 1992. *Organizational Culture and Leadership*, 12–13. San Francisco, CA: Josey-Bass.

Seligman, M. 1990. Learned Optimism, vi–vii. New York, NY: Free Press.

Stogdill, R. 1948. "Personal Factors Associated with Leadership: A Survey of the Literature." *Journal of Psychology* 25, no. 1, pp. 35–71.

The Tailhook Association. 2017. www.tailhook.net

Walsh, J. 2011. "Why the ICC Likely Won't Charge Pope Over Catholic Church Sex Abuses" www.csmonitor.com/World/Europe/2011/0915/Why-the-ICC-likely-won-t-charge-pope-over-Catholic-Church-sex-abuses

Weiss, A. 1994. *Best-Laid Plans*, 112. Shakopee, MN: Las Brisas Research Press.

Wilson, J., and G. Kelling. 1982. "Broken Windows." *Atlantic Monthly* 249, no. 3, pp. 29–38.

Index

Achievement, 170–172
Actions, 24–25
Amazon, 112
Ambiguity, 126
Anna Karenina (Tolstoy), 3
Anna Karenina principle, 3
Authority, 98–99
Avocational section, 120

Bad calls, 131–138. *See also* Touch calls
BAR. *See* Beliefs, Actions, and Results
Being repulsive, 56
Beliefs, Actions, and Results (BAR), 24
Benchmark, 121
Boredom, 168–169
Brainwashing, 90–92
Broken window theory, 101
Burn-Out section, 120
Business-casual ethics, 97–99

Change
    4 P's of change, 158
    "crossing the Rubicon," 146–148
    E's of change approach, 154
    expectations, 148–150
    impact of smallest, 144–146
    leading through stages, 150–155
    preventing, 155–158
Coaching clever people, 46–49
Competing on Analytics: The New Science of Winning (Davenport and Harris), 131
Consistency and commitment, 98
Corporate beliefs, 24
Corporate culture, 5
Counting, 116–118
Creating/Changing organizations, 49–51
Customer/market needs, 100

Davenport, Thomas H., 131
Decisions, 25

Decisiveness, 127
Descriptive model, 125
Drive (Pink), 175

Ego, 163
E's of change approach, 154
Espoused beliefs *vs.* operating beliefs, 34–37
Ethics, business-casual, 97–99

F^2 leadership model, 86–90, 125–126
Fear factors, 28–30
Firmness and Fairness, 86–90
Flexibility, 152–153
Fortitude, 8–10
Fortitude factors, 30–34
4 P's of change, 158

Generationalism, 167
Gilbert, Daniel, 89
Great leaders *vs.* organizational judgment, 128–131
Groupthink, 101
Gyroscope, 6–7

Harris, Jeanne G., 131
Health psychology, 165
Humor, 69–70, 78–82

Id, 163
Inclusion, 98
Inclusive fitness, 99
In-house humor, 69

Judgment, 8–10
Jung, Carl, 65

Kin selection theory, 99

Leading through change, 150
Learning culture, 25
Le Brea Tar Pits, 1
Linda's ten things, 57–63

INDEX

Maister, David, 115
Majoring in the minors, 113–116
McMichael, William, 135
Method of sale/distribution, 111–112
Moral gyroscope, 7
The Mother of All Hooks (McMichael), 135
Motivation, 161–175
Mysterium Coniunctionis (Jung), 65

"Nature/nurture" controversy, 124

One-Hit-Wonder section, 119–120
Operating beliefs *vs.* espoused beliefs, 34–37
Organizational ambidexterity
  customer/market needs, 100
  definition of, 109
  method of sale/distribution, 111–112
  product development, 109–110
  production capability, 110–111
  strategic forces, 109–112
Organizational gladiators, 144
Organizational judgment
  culture of, 130
  definition of, 123
  vs. great leaders, 128–131
Organizational powerhouse, 2

Peer pressure and persuasion, 99–103
Persuasion
  peer pressure and, 99–103
  weapons of mass, 92–97
Pink, Daniel, 175
Powerhouse, 51–56
Prescriptive model, 125
Problem-solving, 151
Product development, 109–110
Production capability, 110–111

Rapport, 98
Raynor, Michael, 109
Reciprocity, 98
Relationships, 152
Relevance, 118–121
Repatriated prisoner of war (RPOW), 75

RPOW. *See* Repatriated prisoner of war

Scarcity, 99
Self-esteem, 38–43
Simplistic *vs.* simple, 101
Smart people, 71–74
Stages of change, 148
Strategy and the Fat Smoker (Maister), 115
The Strategy Paradox (Raynor), 109
Stumbling on Happiness (Gilbert), 89
Superego, 163

Tailhook, 131
"Task Force to Promote Self-Esteem and Personal and Social Responsibility" (Vasconcellos), 38
TCQ. *See* Tough call quotient
"Tip-of-the-iceberg" theory, 162
Titanic disaster, 137
Touch calls
  being repulsive, 56
  believing about opposite, 26–28
  coaching clever people, 46–49
  creating/changing organizations, 49–51
  espoused beliefs *vs.* operating beliefs, 34–37
  experience, 8–10
  fear factors, 28–30
  fortitude, 8–10
  fortitude factors, 30–34
  humor with, 69–70, 78–82
  judgment, 8–10
  Linda's ten things, 57–63
  moral gyroscope, 6–7
  motivation, 161–175
  powerhouse, creating, 51–56
  predicament, 16–18
  results orientation, 10–12
  self-esteem, 38–43
  signs for, 13–16
  taking risks, 24–26
  trusting people, 76–78
Tough call quotient (TCQ), 177–179

Trait, 124–125
Trusting people, 76–78

Unintended consequences, 131–138
Universal traits, 124

Vasconcellos, John, 38
Vietnam Conflict, 66

Vietnam prisoners of war (VPOWs), 66, 68, 71, 73, 76
VPOWs. *See* Vietnam prisoners of war

Washington Post, 137
Weapons of mass persuasion, 92–97
Working together, 42–43

OTHER TITLES IN THE HUMAN RESOURCE MANAGEMENT AND ORGANIZATIONAL BEHAVIOR COLLECTION

- *The Illusion of Inclusion: Global Inclusion, Unconscious Bias, and the Bottom Line* by Helen Turnbull
- *On All Cylinders: The Entrepreneur's Handbook* by Ron Robinson
- *Employee LEAPS: Leveraging Engagement by Applying Positive Strategies* by Kevin E. Phillips
- *Making Human Resource Technology Decisions: A Strategic Perspective* by Janet H. Marler and Sandra L. Fisher
- *Feet to the Fire: How to Exemplify And Create The Accountability That Creates Great Companies* By Lorraine A. Moore
- *HR Analytics and Innovations in Workforce Planning* By Tony Miller
- *Deconstructing Management Maxims, Volume I: A Critical Examination of Conventional Business Wisdom* by Kevin Wayne
- *Deconstructing Management Maxims, Volume II: A Critical Examination of Conventional Business Wisdom* by Kevin Wayne
- *The Real Me: Find and Express Your Authentic Self* by Mark Eyre
- *Across the Spectrum: What Color Are You?* by Stephen Elkins-Jarrett
- *The Human Resource Professional's Guide to Change Management: Practical Tools and Techniques to Enact Meaningful and Lasting Organizational Change* by Melanie J. Peacock

Announcing the Business Expert Press Digital Library

Concise e-books business students need for classroom and research

This book can also be purchased in an e-book collection by your library as

- a one-time purchase,
- that is owned forever,
- allows for simultaneous readers,
- has no restrictions on printing, and
- can be downloaded as PDFs from within the library community.

Our digital library collections are a great solution to beat the rising cost of textbooks. E-books can be loaded into their course management systems or onto students' e-book readers.
The **Business Expert Press** digital libraries are very affordable, with no obligation to buy in future years. For more information, please visit **www.businessexpertpress.com/librarians**. To set up a trial in the United States, please email **sales@businessexpertpress.com**.

CPSIA information can be obtained
at www.ICGtesting.com
Printed in the USA
FFOW02n0441220917
40121FF